THE FORMATIVE ERA OF AMERICAN LAW

THE FORMATIVE ERA OF AMERICAN LAW

by

ROSCOE POUND

GLOUCESTER, MASS.
PETER SMITH

*Reprinted, 1960, by special arrangement
with Little, Brown and Company, Inc.*

PRINTED IN THE UNITED STATES OF AMERICA

To

RUFUS E. FOSTER

United States Circuit Judge for the Fifth Circuit

IVRIS VTRIVSQVE PERITVS

PREFACE

THESE four lectures are printed as they were delivered at the Law School of Tulane University on the occasion of the centennial of the death of Edward Livingston, October 27–30, 1936. I have added some notes intended for the most part to illustrate or explain the points made.

It would take a book running into a number of volumes to set forth adequately the history of the formative era of American law. Nor is the time ripe for such a book. Too much preliminary work remains to be done in local legal history in almost every state and locality. But it is possible from the reports, statutes, and text books, to trace the working of the juristic theory which was chiefly operative, and to outline the development and achievements of the chief agencies of legal development in that era. Nothing more has been attempted.

As I am telling of the reception, adaptation and developing of a taught legal tradition, it has been necessary to say something about recent theories of law as formulated class self-interest, or as a product of individual judicial psychology governing the behavior of the judge, or as a disappearing phenomenon in the society of the future.

ROSCOE POUND

Harvard Law School
July 13, 1938

INTRODUCTION

BY RUFUS C. HARRIS
President of Tulane University

AS POLITICAL and ideological heir of Jefferson, definitely appointed by Jefferson in a letter which might be called a political testament, and as the theorist behind Andrew Jackson, Edward Livingston has an importance for the international movement that founded American democracy which cannot be overstated. Jackson's nullification proclamation is usually attributed to Livingston and its nationalism was laid to the "metaphysics of the Montesquieu of the cabinet." Livingston transformed Jefferson's democratic localism into democratic nationalism, so that we are justified in seeing a line of intellectual succession in Jefferson, Livingston, and Jackson.

But his great contribution was leadership of the codification movement. This, too, was based on his democratic conceptions. No one emphasized more the relation between democracy and codification.

INTRODUCTION

This volume is the salute by the great American jurist of our time to the great American jurist of our earliest period. The occasion was the centenary of the death of Edward Livingston. At the invitation of the Faculty of Law of Tulane University, under whose patronage the centennial program was held, Mr. Pound gave four lectures at the Tulane College of Law, now published in this volume. The Faculty of Law, which in so many different ways is bound to Mr. Pound, was honored that he took the occasion of the Livingston Centennial to give the first serious and the first comprehensive account of the formative period of American legal history.

CONTENTS

THE FORMATIVE ERA OF AMERICAN LAW

I

NATURAL LAW

WHEN we celebrate the hundredth anniversary of Livingston's death, we are very near to celebrating the centennial of the formative era of American law. If we think of that era as extending from independence to the time of the Civil War, it was three quarters of its way by 1836. The legal portions of our Constitutions, state and federal, were what they were to be until the amendments to the federal Constitution after the Civil War, and substantially what they were to be till the end of the nineteenth century. The legislative reform movement was well under way both in England and with us. New York, for example, already had elaborate modern statutes as to corporations, wills and administration, descent and distribution, marriage and divorce, executions against real property, real property, and criminal law.[1] Kent's work for American equity was at an end. Marshall had died a year before. Story and Gibson had each been on the bench nearly a quarter of a century. François Xavier Martin had sat for over twenty years on the Supreme Court of Louisiana. Blackford had been for a decade on the highest court of Indiana. Shaw and Ruffin were well established in their long and fruitful judicial careers. Thus, of the ten judges who must be ranked first in American judicial history,[2] six had done their enduring work before the Civil War, and indeed had done the most of it in the first third of the one hundred and fifty years that have elapsed since the Federal Constitution. Of the great lawyers of the period before the Civil War, Luther Martin, after two generations at the head of the profession, and William Pinkney and William Wirt, after a generation of leadership, were dead. Jeremiah Mason had been forty-five years at the bar. Daniel Webster and Horace Binney had each been a generation at the bar and Webster had already argued many of the great cases which made our constitutional law. Reverdy Johnson had been two decades at the bar and Rufus Choate was well established in the profession. The Litchfield Law School had come to an end and in place of the apprentice type of training for which it stood, the academic type which was to prevail had been definitely set up with the prestige of Story behind it.[3] Also the text writing, which was to be an element of the first importance in our legal development in this period, had become well under way with the work of Kent and Story and Reeve and Gould and Tucker. Not the least of the great names of this classical era is that of Livingston.

Livingston was, indeed, typical of the strong lawyers and enlightened statesmen who made this era classical. He shows in every connection the faith in reason which was characteristic of the period and was in large part the source of its strength. While the science of law upon the Continent was coming to hold that nothing could be achieved by conscious, intelligent, juristic effort, he had no doubt of its efficacy. Most of all he was, like all the jurists of the school of natural law, a man of action where the jurists of the later nineteenth century were exclusively men of reflection. Grotius had a wholly diplomatic and political career. Montesquieu's career was wholly political. Vattel's activities were entirely diplomatic and political. Burlamaqui taught but incidentally in a political career. Blackstone's lectures at Oxford were but an episode in the life of a lawyer and judge. Kent and Story spent the best part of their lives in judicial office. If Pufendorf and Wolff were teachers, none the less they had stormy careers because they would meddle in politics. Livingston, who was successively District Attorney, Member of Congress, United States Senator, Member of President Jackson's Cabinet, and

Minister to France, belongs in this category. If we compare these men with the academic teachers of the historical school, Savigny, Maine, and in this country, Ames and Thayer and Bigelow, it is not difficult to see why it was that the latter believed law could only be found by historical study, distrusted legislation, and were averse to action, while the former did not doubt they could achieve lasting results by exercise of their powers of reason, taught principles of constructive lawmaking, and believed in action.

Let us recall the task of the formative era. The common law as the colonists knew it was the law of the age of Coke, not the law of the age of Mansfield. It was heavily burdened with the formalism of the strict law. Its ideals were those of the relationally organized society of the Middle Ages and so quite out of line with the needs and ideas of men who were opening up the wilderness. It spoke from an era of organization while the colonists represented an oncoming era of individualism. But there was little need for law until the economic development of the colonies and the rise of trade and commerce in the eighteenth century. Then there began to be trained lawyers practising in the courts and courts manned by trained lawyers, so that the reception of the common law and reshaping it into a law for America were well begun at the time of the Revolution. The Revolution, however, and its results in the years immediately following, set back this development for a time and led to a critical period in the history of our law. The conservatism characteristic of lawyers led many of the strongest men at the bar to take the royalist side and decimated the profession. A deep and widespread economic depression set in. Business had been wholly deranged. The ports had been closed and trade cut off. Enormous public debts required ruinous taxation. It was an era of strict foreclosure and imprisonment for debt.[4] For a generation after the Revolution, law and lawyers suffered from the ill effects of this period of depression. Moreover, political conditions gave rise to a general distrust of English law. Naturally the public was very hostile to England and to all that was English, and it was impossible for the common law to escape the odium of its origin. The books are full of illustrations of the hostility toward English law simply because it was English which prevailed at the end of the eighteenth and in the earlier years of the nineteenth century.[5]

Social and geographical conditions contributed also to make the work of receiving and reshaping the common law exceptionally difficult. The idea of a profession was repugnant to the Jeffersonian era. The feeling was strong that all callings should be on the same footing. To dignify one by calling it a profession, and to prescribe qualifications for and limit access to it, seemed undemocratic and un-American. All the states came to make entrance to the profession easy with a minimum of qualification.[6] Geographical conditions completed the process of decentralizing the law and deprofessionalizing the lawyers. In a country of long distances and a time of slow and expensive travel, the common law system of central courts and a centralized bar imposed an intolerable burden upon litigants.[7] For a time there was a veritable cult of local law.[8]

It was the task of our formative era, in the face of these difficulties, to work out from our inherited legal materials a general body of law for what was to be a politically and economically unified land.

A word as to these materials. We may look at them conveniently as they stood in 1774 at the time of the Declaration of Rights of the Continental Congress. In this declaration the common law of England is asserted as the measure of the rights of Americans and applicability to American conditions is declared to be the test by which English legal precepts were to be judged.[9] But it was not easy in the colonies to find out what that law was. Of forty-eight law books listed by Dr. James [10] as published in the colonies before 1775, thirty-six are pertinent to our subject. The rest are editions or translations of Beccaria, accounts of the trial of Zenger, and the like. Of the thirty-six, seven have to do with the rights of Englishmen (mostly on the basis of Coke's Second Institute), twelve with constables and sheriffs, five with justices of the peace, three are clerks' manuals, one treats of grand juries, one of courts martial, and one is a manual for county and town officers. Three hand books for laymen (of the Every Man his own Lawyer type), an edition of Blackstone (two of book 4), and a treatise on pleading, are all that have to do with the securing of personality and substance which are the staple of the lawyer's work. For practical purposes Coke's Second Institute and Blackstone are the repositories of the law.

A like story is told by the law reports of the time. Only three reporters have cases of this period, Dallas, Jefferson, and Quincy. But 1 Dallas was published in 1790, Jefferson in 1829, and Quincy in 1865. There simply were no generally accessible reports of decisions of American courts until the nineteenth century. Moreover, the decisions themselves down to 1775 have to do with a very narrow field. Of thirty-three cases in 1 Dallas (from 1743 to 1774) seventeen are on points of evidence, three on real property, three on civil procedure, three on criminal procedure, two on pleading, and three on what English statutes were in force in Colonial

Pennsylvania. One case on sales, one on equitable conversion, and two on customary modes of conveyancing in the colony, have some bearing on the law of the future. In Jefferson's reports, three fourths of the cases have to do with slavery. The rest relate to the old law of real property or to the law of the state church. In Quincy's reports, two thirds of the cases have to do with the technicalities of the old common-law practice and most of the rest go on the old technical land law. One case on bills and notes has to do with what we should regard today as living law. Once more we are left to Blackstone, with his complacent view of the feudal real property law, over-refined procedure, and seventeenth-century equity in which he had been brought up, as things complete and final, needing only a bit of tinkering here and there.[11]

Trade and commerce, with resulting development of equity and of the law merchant, had done much to liberalize the common-law system by the end of the eighteenth century and the industrial revolution was to make it over in the nineteenth century. But the crystallizing of equity and absorption of the law merchant were not complete in England when we became independent and the industrial revolution was almost complete in nineteenth-century England before it began with us. In our social development we begin with a pioneer society struggling to subdue the wilderness and defend against the Indians. Then follows a time of settled agriculture, an era of small towns. Upon this follows a period of commercial progress, involving the rise of seaport cities and trade centers. Then comes industrial supremacy and the rise of great metropolitan centers. Some of these stages have followed rapidly at times and in places and more slowly in others. The second and third overlap in the older states; the third follows more slowly in the West. The fourth is wholly achieved in some parts of the land, hardly at all in others. There are still areas definitely in the second stage. Thus the pressure in our formative era came partly from the needs of a pioneer society, impatient of forms and eager to cut across technical procedural lines and modes of conveyancing and requisites of transactions, and partly from the exigencies of trade and commerce.

As to the pioneer contribution, Mr. Justice Miller is reported to have said that a prime factor in shaping the law in our western states was ignorance: The first judges "did not know enough to do the wrong thing, so they did the right thing." [12] As to the effect of expanding trade and commerce, Plato had noted that where there is maritime commerce there must be more law.[13] Montesquieu, observing the phenomena of his time, says that in a trading city there are more laws.[14] Jhering, in a characteristically eloquent passage, speaks of commerce as a pathfinder in legal history.[15] The classical period of Roman law, the no less classical period of the modern Roman law, the era of the development of equity and of the law merchant in England, and the formative period of American law all bear abundant witness to this.

In our formative era, some relied on rational overhauling of the legal materials at hand. Others urged that we make a complete legal new start; that we set up an American code out of whole cloth, just as today, in a new creative era, there are jurists who would start over again on a wholly new basis. But most lawyers sought to reshape or add to the existing stock of authoritative legal materials, just as today, for the most part, we would make over what has come down to us from the last century with the aid of a social philosophy and in the light of the social sciences. But whether they thought to make over or to build anew, the lawyers and judges and teachers of the formative era found their creating and organizing idea in the theory of natural law. This idea, at work in legislation (for in the maturity of law legislation is the chief instrument of change, and this was the time of the legislative reform movement both in England and in America), in judicial decision, and in doctrinal writing, guided the creative process of applying reason to experience which has been the life of the law.

Although speculation as to natural law is to be found in the theological philosophical writings of the Middle Ages, it becomes significant for the law at and after the Reformation and becomes dominant in juristic thought in the seventeenth century. A perennial problem of the legal order is to reconcile the need of stability with the inevitableness of change.[16] In practice, this reconciliation is achieved by means of ideals, to which lawmaking and interpretation and judicial application and doctrinal development tend to conform. These ideals give direction to change. They lead to change, but they guide it, and, as they are applied to authoritative legal materials shaped by the past, and as the ideals are of necessity largely ideal conceptions of the society and institutions and legal precepts with which lawmaker or judge or jurist is familiar, they tend to maintain stability during change.

A Greek city state was a politically organized society. But much of its ethical custom and law spoke from an older kin-organized society. There was a competition between a traditional tribal law and the politically enacted law of the city state. Philosophers began to think about this and about the great diversity of customs and laws both as between Greeks and barbarians and as between Greek cities themselves. Wide commercial intercourse with all peoples showed that no two were alike in these respects, and experience taught that the same Greek city often had different bodies of legal precepts at different times. Hence some inferred that the legal and moral orders were mere matters of enactment or convention and so that the legal order was subject to the arbitrary control of those who wielded political power for the time being.[17] Yet, in view of the struggles of oligarchy and democracy for political supremacy which were the staple of life in the classical Greek city, this conception was not satisfying from the standpoint of the general security. Accordingly other philosophers looked for some assured basis of social control other than tradition and habit of obedience or the will of the politically supreme for the moment. They saw such a basis in the uniform and universal phenomena of physical nature. The social and legal orders were likened to the natural order.[18] Right and law had their basis in a harmony or fitness involved in the nature of things. They were independent of human will and had universal validity.[19] Thus Greek philosophers distinguished the just by nature (*i.e.* just in ideal) from the just by convention and enactment.[20] From the just by nature Roman lawyers came to the conception of law by nature.[21] Ever since, systems of legal ideals have gone by the name of natural law.

Dissolution of relationally organized society, discovery of the new world, creating individual opportunities and setting free individual enterprise to exploit the resources of nature, the boundless faith in reason which had come with the Renaissance, and the breakdown of authoritative interpretation at the Reformation, contributed to overthrow the universal, stable law taught by the medieval universities. Morals were set free from authority.[22] Philosophy emancipated itself from Aristotle. Jurisprudence was divorced from theology.[23] Law was detached from the Corpus Juris.[24] Yet men felt the need of an unchallengeable starting point as much as ever. They believed they had found it in reason. Reason demonstrating and expressed in natural law replaced authority.[25]

This natural law was variously conceived: sometimes as a vaguely outlined ideal order of society,[26] sometimes as a body of moral ideals to which conduct should be constrained to conform,[27] sometimes as a body of ideal legal precepts by which the precepts of positive law are to be criticized and to which, so far as possible, they are to be made to conform.[28] But whatever meaning was given to the ideal or body of ideals, the interpretation and application of existing rules were to be guided by it, and lawmaking, judicial reasoning, and doctrinal writing were to be governed by it.[29]

At least in the modern world, natural law has always had two sides: a side making for change, a creative side, and a side making for stability, a systematizing, organizing side. From the very beginning of the school of natural law in the sixteenth century and throughout its hegemony in the seventeenth and eighteenth centuries, the two sides clearly stand out—natural law as an instrument of change, as a weapon in the attack on the authoritarianism of the Middle Ages, and natural law as an insurer of stability, as a protection from the personal justice and arbitrary administration of an era in which the old authoritative restraints were giving way and absolute governments had become established.

Livingston understood the nature and function of the theory of natural law very much better than Bentham. Bentham frequently uses "natural" in this connection in the sense of primitive as distinguished from man-made or artificial.[30] Thus, in his treatise on legislation he says that to speak of natural law is a contradiction in terms, since laws are required precisely because it is needful to repress men's natural inclinations. The most repressive laws, he says, have to be made against these natural inclinations.[31] But obviously such laws are not called for as a check upon men's ideal inclinations. In another place Bentham speaks of nature as making such and such a law and of natural law as "presenting us with the will of an unknown legislator as being in itself authoritative." [32] Here Bentham looks at the theory of natural law from a political standpoint. To him law presupposes a lawgiver—a political lawmaking authority. But the law-of-nature school looked at it from a moral standpoint. They thought of a moral duty to do what the moral ideal indicated and of the precept of the political lawgiver as an attempt to realize that ideal. Livingston understood this. Indeed, Livingston is likely to be more appreciated in the revival of natural law which has been going on all over the world in response to a demand for liberalisation of law in a changing social and economic order.[33]

In studying the formative era of American law we are concerned immediately with the eighteenth-century natural law which became embodied for us in the Declaration of Independence and is behind our bills of rights. But this natural law is only a development of what we find in Grotius, and already in Grotius we find the two methods which the eighteenth century jurists did not succeed in reconciling, namely, on the one hand recourse to constructive ideals, drawn from reason and used as agencies of creative change, and on the other hand resort to a presumption that legal precepts which obtain generally over the civilized world are declaratory of reason.[34] The latter gradually gains the day as the creative work of the formative era is achieved. The creative theory becomes a theory of justifying, not one of constructing. Here, I need not say, we come once more to a pervading problem of jurisprudence, the balance between stability and change. The controversy as to the type of law, whether custom or common law or tradition, on the one hand, or legislation, on the other, the controversy as to the relation of law to morals, the discussion as between adjudication and administration, as between law and equity, as between strict and free procedure, all run back to this problem of stability and change, and so to the fundamental one of a balance between the general security and the individual life.[35] Either of these may furnish the ideal for a system of natural law, as each has furnished at one time or another a received, authoritative ideal held and applied as part of the positive law.

Three ideals and resulting canons of value for the recognition, delimitation, and securing of interests have obtained in juristic thought. One looks at all things from the standpoint of the individual human personality. It regards state and law as existing only to guarantee the security and development of the individual. Civilization gets its significance as a means of educating the individual. The highest end is individual freedom. A second looks at all things from the standpoint of organized society. It reckons personality values and civilization values in terms of community values or political values. The significant values are collective values. Morals and civilization are means toward the purposes of the state. The highest end is the nation or state. A third regards the first two as transcended in the conception of civilization and the values of civilized life. It reckons personality values and community values in terms of civilization values. Individual self-assertion, spontaneous individual initiative and free individual activity, on the one hand, and co-operation and planned collective activity, on the other hand, are thought of as means toward or agencies of civilization. Morals, law, and the state get their significance as making for civilization. The highest end is civilization.[36] In the formative era of American law the first of these ideals was received and became authoritative. But natural law is not tied to the individualist ideal for all time. Today the second and the third are contesting. The adherents of the second take the Marxian view that law will disappear with private property in the classless state. The adherents of the third, or many of them, tend to set up a new natural law.

In the ferment following independence, in the finding of a law for the new world, in the working out of bodies of law for the new commonwealths which grew up so fast in the course of our westward expansion across the continent, the creative side of natural law was resorted to by legislators, judges, and text writers. The system of equity was not yet complete in England and absorption of the law merchant was still going forward. Much of the seventeenth-century law was in the condition in which it had come down from the Middle Ages. The criminal law of Blackstone's time was full of archaisms and the penal system was almost untouched by the humane ideas of the classical penologists. The legislative reform movement began here rather than in England.[37] Our courts had to complete the development of equity and the taking over of the law merchant concurrently with the English courts. Legislatures and courts and doctrinal writers had to test the common law at every point with respect to its applicability to America. Judges and doctrinal writers had to develop an American common law, a body of judicially declared or doctrinally approved precepts suitable to America, out of the old English cases and the old English statutes. They did this, and did it thoroughly, in about three quarters of a century. No other judicial and juristic achievement may be found to compare with this. However much the last generation may have railed at the theory of natural law, no achievements of any of its theories are at all comparable.

With the rise of historical thinking in the nineteenth century there comes to be a combination of history and philosophy, observable in Kent and marked in Story.[88] The stabilizing work of natural law is taken over by history, after history has for a time reinforced reason as reason in the later Middle Ages had bolstered up authority. Before this, in the later eighteenth century the creative force of natural law tended to be spent. There was in Europe a tendency to stagnation of thought until, as Kant put it, philosophy awoke from a dogmatic slumber. There is nothing of consequence in the English eighteenth-century text, Rutherforth's Institutes of Natural Law, which is not in Grotius. Bentham's utilitarianism has nothing in it which was not in the utilitarian natural law which went before him except his calculus of pains and pleasures. The proposition that the end sought by man is happiness, as a proposition of natural law shown by reason, goes back to Pufendorf and may be found in Rutherforth, Burlamaqui and Vattel.[89] But a political idea, a proposition that what every one agrees to is declaratory of natural law, a consensual natural law, as it were, is manifest in much American writing on natural law,[40] where the historical idea is to be seen in the pages of Kent and Story. Yet this consensual idea, reminiscent of the Roman juristic identification of the *jus gentium* with the *jus naturale*, may be found in Grotius. He says in effect that whatever cannot be deduced from certain principles by a sure process of reasoning, and yet is clearly observed everywhere, must have a natural origin in consent.[41] Men were morally, ideally, and so legally bound by their free consent. Thus in Grotius we have a theory available to check institutional waste, as the historical theory was used in the latter part of the nineteenth century, and in Grotius we have also a purely systematizing theory, to be much used in the maturity of our law. "For," says he, "the principles of the law of nature, since they are always the same, can easily be brought into systematic form; but the elements of positive law, since they often undergo changes and are different in different places, are outside the domain of systematic treatment." [42]

In the nineteenth century the stabilizing and conserving natural law takes on three forms, ethical, political, and economic. The ethical form,[43] in which moral precepts dictated by reason are the ideal, is the oldest, coming from the seventeenth century, where it connects with the theological natural law of the Middle Ages. It is replaced in early nineteenth-century America by the political form in which an ideal of "the nature of American institutions" or the "nature of free institutions" [44] or the "nature of free government" [45] is the starting point. Later, as the stabilizing side of natural law comes to be the one stressed chiefly, an economic ideal of a society ordered by the principles of the classical political economy prevails.[46] This form soon merges in the nineteenth-century historical-metaphysical thinking which puts free individual self-assertion as the end of the legal order.[47] The excesses of this type of thinking in the maturity of our law had much to do with the discredit in the last generation of what had been the guiding mode of thought of our great legislators and great judges and great text writers. Perhaps because his main interest was in penal legislation, where there was still work for the ethical type, there is little of the political and none of the economic natural law in Livingston's pages.[48]

If we ask what were the results of natural-law thinking in the three generations after independence, in which it held the field undisputed in this country, we must put on the bad side of the account its effect on American attempts at codification in the nineteenth century. Undue confidence in the power of individual reason to discover the right rule led to neglect of history and, what was worse, to expecting too much of a single codifier.[49] On this side, too, we must put the absolute idea of law which prevailed with us so largely in the last century and the wide gulf between popular thinking and professional thinking as to social legislation to which it led. This idea came to us from Grotius in two ways. On the one hand it came through Blackstone, whose section "on the nature of laws in general" is founded on Grotius and Pufendorf.[50] On the other hand, it comes through American publicists in the eighteenth and nineteenth centuries who followed the Dutch and French publicists and civilians. Thus in Wilson's Law Lectures (1791) Pufendorf is cited twenty-nine times and there are ten references to Grotius, ten to Vattel, four to Burlamaqui, and five to Rutherforth's Institutes of Natural Law, an exposition of Grotius. Again, in the first volume of Story on the Constitution, there are nineteen citations of Vattel, six of Heineccius, three of Burlamaqui, two of Grotius, and two of Rutherforth.

We must remember that these books and others of the sort were the staple of the beginnings of American legal education. This goes back of the Revolution. Gridley, the "father of the Boston bar," Attorney-General of Massachusetts in 1742, was the American legal scholar of the time. When John Adams was studying law, Gridley told him that a lawyer in this part of the world had more to learn than an English lawyer. "A lawyer in this country," he said, "must study common law and civil law and natural law and admiralty law." [51] The civil law, natural law and admiralty were not studied in the Inns of Court at that time. Writing in 1760, Adams tells us that he had read two Dutch commentators on the Institutes of Justinian and had Grotius and Pufendorf yet to read.[52] About the same time one of the then leaders of the New York bar laid out a course of study in which, of nine general works, the first three were Wood's Institutes of the Civil Law, Domat's Civil Law and Pufendorf.[53] In 1778 a course of study laid out by Judge William Parker, leader of the bar in New Hampshire, includes Burlamaqui and Pufendorf, then translated into English.[54] In 1788, when John Quincy Adams began to read law, Theophilus Parsons, afterward Chief Justice of Massachusetts, gave him a list of books to be read of which the second is Vattel.[55] In 1779, James Kent began with Blackstone and then read Grotius and Pufendorf.[56] Daniel Webster in 1804 read Vattel for the third time.[57] Blackstone continued to be the student's first work in the law office and in most law schools until the end of the nineteenth century, and select chapters from Grotius and Pufendorf were in law school curricula until 1850.[58]

With the advent of historical and analytical jurisprudence in American legal thought after the Civil War, there was little patience with the ideas of the seventeenth and eighteenth centuries. It became the fashion to sneer at the great law writers of the formative era of our law. Even Gray attributes the decision in Swift *v.* Tyson not to Story's conception of natural law but to fondness for generalities and restless vanity.[59] We should not forget that the last four decades of the nineteenth century in the United States and the last half of the century on the Continent called for organization and system and stability, after an era of legal growth, rather than for creation and change. For a season philosophy had done its work. Today there is a revival of interest in the seventeenth and eighteenth centuries as we realize that we have the same problem of liberalizing and reshaping and supplementing a traditional body of authoritative legal materials which confronted them.

Discredit of natural law in this generation is due chiefly to its effects in our constitutional law. In the last of its phases it led to a notion of the Constitution as declaratory of natural law and so of an ideal of the common law as in its main lines and characteristic doctrines an embodiment of universal precepts running back of all constitutions. Thus certain common-law doctrines and traditionally received ideals of the profession were made into a super-constitution by which the social legislation of the last decade of the nineteenth century and of the first third of the present century was to be judged.[60]

On the other side of the account we must set down that the believers in eighteenth-century natural law did great things in the development of American law because that theory gave faith that they could do them. Application of reason to the details of the received common law was what made the work of the legislative reform movement of enduring worth. Some of its best achievements were in formulating authoritatively what men had reasoned out in the era of the school of the law of nature in the seventeenth and eighteenth centuries. Yet it has to its credit also more than one independent bit of creative lawmaking such as we had not had at the hands of later legislators down to the Workmen's Compensation Laws.[61]

Today rationalism is under attack from another quarter. A psychological realism is abroad which regards reason as affording no more than a cover of illusion for processes judicial and administrative which are fundamentally and necessarily unrational. But merely destructive so-called realism makes neither for stability nor for change since it gives us nothing in place of what it would take away. Civilisation involves a harnessing of internal no less than of external nature to men's use. Hence in the progress of civilisation there is a progressive tying down of those nonrational tendencies in the behavior of judges and magistrates and administrative agencies upon which the realist of today puts so much emphasis.[62] If reason is not all-sufficient to achieve this conquest of internal nature, as the eighteenth century assumed it was, yet it has done much and it can do more. It needs supplementing not rejecting. Jurists of the law-of-nature school were not wholly in error in insisting that appeal to the conscience of the citizen, appeal to his reason, was the foundation of the authority of the legal order and so of the precepts of a body of laws. Habits of obedience give way unless they have this support of reason. The social psychological guarantee of which Jellinek speaks[63] is fortified by reason. If reason sometimes comes to the aid of the anti-social, by and large reasoned reflection upon experience is a bulwark of society.

Today the role of the ideal element in law and the need of a canon of values and technique of applying it are recognized by all except those who still cling to nineteenth-century analytical jurisprudence and take it to be the whole of the science of law, and those skeptical realists who take the judicial and administrative processes, determined by individual psychology, as all that is significant. Natural law, as it is revived today, seeks to organize the ideal element in law, to furnish a critique of old received ideals and give a basis for formulating new ones, and to yield a reasoned canon of values and a technique of applying it. I should prefer to call it philosophical jurisprudence. But one can well sympathize with those who would salvage the good will of the old name as an asset of the science of law.

In setting forth the claims of the revived natural law of today, I am not holding a brief for the old natural law. I should not for a moment urge jurists to return to the mode of thought of the eighteenth century. But we need to understand it if we would understand how our law came to be what it is. Austin speaks of it as "naught."[64] Yet *ex nihilo nihil fit.* A mode of thought which produced and developed the classical international law, which modernized the civil law so that it could go round the world, which had much influence on the development of equity and the law merchant — the liberalizing agencies in the Anglo-American common law — which was the theoretical basis of much of the best work of Lord Mansfield, of the Declaration of Independence and bills of rights, and of the legislation, judicial decision, and doctrinal writing of the formative era of American law, is not to be rated as nothing in legal history. If we concede the failure of the old natural law to come up to the more rigorous requirements of nineteenth-century thought in the wake of Kant, and whatever we may feel as to its intrinsic nothingness, no one can say truthfully that it wrought nothing.

[1] New York, Revised Stat., 2 ed. (1836), vol. I, 591 (1819), II, 373 (1832), III, 220 (1811); *id.* II, 2 (1827); *id.* II, 23 (1823); *id.* I, 741 (1827), II, 32 (1823); *id.* II, 74 (1830); *id.* II, 288 (1828); *id.* I, 713 (1828); *id.* II, 545 (1828).

[2] In chronological order they are: John Marshall (1755–1835, Chief Justice of the United States for thirty-four years, 1801–1835), James Kent (1763–1847, on the bench for twenty-five years, 1798–1823, Justice of the Supreme Court of New York six years, Chief Justice ten years, and thereafter Chancellor of New York for nine years), Joseph Story (1779–1845, for thirty-two years a Justice of the Supreme Court of the United States), John Bannister Gibson (1780–1853, a judge for forty years, 1813–1853, three years on the Pennsylvania Court of Common Pleas, thirty-seven years in the Supreme Court of Pennsylvania, twenty-three of them as Chief Justice), Lemuel Shaw (1781–1861, for thirty-one years, 1830–1861, Chief Justice of Massachusetts), Thomas Ruffin (1787–1870, on the bench thirty-five years, 1818–1853, nine years as judge of the Superior Court of North Carolina, seven years as Justice of the Supreme Court of that state, and nineteen years as Chief Justice), Thomas McIntyre Cooley (1824–1898, for twenty-one years a judge of the Supreme Court of Michigan, 1864–1885, and for four years, 1887–1891, a member of the Interstate Commerce Commis-

sion, doing pioneer work upon what was to become a model of American administrative tribunals), Charles Doe (1830–1896, on the Supreme Court of New Hampshire thirty-five years, fifteen as a justice and twenty years as Chief Justice), Oliver Wendell Holmes (1841–1935, on the bench fifty years, seventeen years, 1882–1899, a justice of the Supreme Judicial Court of Massachusetts, Chief Justice of that Court for three years, 1899–1902, and Justice of the Supreme Court of the United States thirty years, 1902–1932), Benjamin Nathan Cardozo (1870–1938, Justice of the Supreme Court of New York, 1914–1917, designated to serve as judge of the Court of Appeals 1914, Associate Judge of the Court of Appeals, 1917–1932, after 1932 Justice of the Supreme Court of the United States).

[8] American law schools have a twofold origin, on the one hand, professorships founded in the latter part of the eighteenth century in imitation of Blackstone's chair at Oxford, and on the other hand, law offices in which the preceptor's function developed along with but at the expense of practice of law. Of the former type are the chairs held by Chancellor Wythe at William and Mary (1779–1780), by James Wilson at the College of Philadelphia (1790), and by James Kent at Columbia (1793). The other type begins with Judge Reeve's school at Litchfield, Conn., about 1784. The school which Asahel Stearns set up at Harvard in 1817 was of this sort, but combined with it was the Royall Professorship at Harvard provided for in 1781 but not established till 1815. Change from a professional school under the eaves of a university to an academic professional school came with the appointment of Joseph Story as Dane Professor at Harvard in 1829. After 1848 no teacher holding a law professorship at Harvard attempted to combine teaching with regular, continuous practice of his profession, but elsewhere the conception of a professor of law as a "full-time teacher" made its way slowly. In 1870, Harvard took the further step forward of choosing part of

its law teachers from recent graduates on the basis of scholarship and with reference to their scholarly and teaching promise. In the present century the policy of full-time teachers has come to prevail generally, and the policy of selection on the basis of scholarship, with or without a short experience in practice, has become generally accepted. In the present generation the bulk of the profession came to be trained in such law schools rather than through apprenticeship in the offices of practitioners.

[4] Arrest and imprisonment on civil process at law and on execution in equity founded upon contract were abolished in New York in 1831. Massachusetts substantially abolished arrest and imprisonment for debt by statute in 1834 and 1842. Tennessee abolished imprisonment for debt in 1831, Indiana in 1838, Ohio in 1838, Michigan in 1839, Mississippi in 1839, Vermont in 1839, New Hampshire in 1840, Connecticut in 1842, Pennsylvania in 1842, and New Jersey in 1844. For the Federal Courts it was abolished in 1841.

[5] See Patterson's Laws of New Jersey, 436 (Act of June 13, 1799, § 7); Whitehead, The Supreme Court of New Jersey, 3 Green Bag, 401, 402; Acts of Kentucky, 1807, p. 23 (see preface to 1 Litt. [Ky.]); Corning, The Highest Courts of Law in New Hampshire, 2 Green Bag, 469, 470; Memoirs of Chancellor Kent, 117, 118; Journeymen Cordwainers Case, Yates, Select Cases (N. Y.) 111 (1808); Loyd, Early Courts of Pennsylvania, 150; Sullivan, History of Land Titles in Massachusetts, 337 (1801). Dembitz, Kentucky Jurisprudence, 7, 8.

[6] See Reed, Training for the Public Profession of the Law, 85–93.

[7] See Pound, Organization of Courts, 70 Philadelphia Legal Intelligencer, 86; also in Proc. Minn. Bar Assn. 1914, 169.

[8] See, *e.g.*, the title page of Ebersole, Encyclopedia of Iowa Law (1903).

[9] "Whereupon the deputies so appointed being now as-

sembled in a full and free representation of these colonies, taking into their most serious consideration the best means of attaining the ends aforesaid, do in the first place, as Englishmen, their ancestors, in like cases have usually done, for asserting and vindicating their rights and liberties declare. . . .

5. That the respective colonies are entitled to the common law of England, and more especially to the great and inestimable privilege of being tried by their peers of the vicinage, according to the course of that law.

6. That they are entitled to the benefit of such of the English statutes as existed at the time of their colonization; and which they have, by experience, respectively found to be applicable to their several local and other circumstances." — Declaration of Rights of the Continental Congress (1774).

[10] James, A List of Legal Treatises Printed in the British Colonies and the American States before 1801, in Harvard Legal Essays, 154, 159–178.

[11] 4 Commentaries on the Laws of England, 441–443.

[12] This was a saying generally attributed to him by lawyers who practiced in the federal courts in the Eighth Circuit when I came to the bar (1890).

[13] Plato, Laws, bk. 8, 842.

[14] L'esprit des lois, liv. XX, chap. 18.

[15] "Already in the dawn of history, trade had done a good part of its day's work; while the states fought each other it sought and levelled the ways which lead through one people to another and established among them a relation of exchange of ways and ideas. It was a pathfinder in the wilderness, a herald of peace, a torchbearer of civilization." Zweck im Recht, I, 233.

[16] See Pound, Interpretations of Legal History, 1–11.

[17] *E.g.* Antisthenes, Diogenes Laertius, vi, 1, 2.

[18] *E.g.* in the Pseudo-Platonic Minos. I have discussed this point more fully in Law and Morals, 4–6.

[19] *E.g.* Chrysippus, Diogenes Laertius, vii, 98.

[20] Aristotle, Nicomachean Ethics, V, 7.

[21] See Voigt, Das Jus naturale, aequum et bonum und Jus Gentium der Römer, I, 273–4.

[22] Hemmingius (Hemmingsen), De lege naturae apodictica methodus, chap. 2.

[23] *Ibid.*; Grotius, De iure belli ac pacis, prolegomena, § 11.

[24] Hotman, Anti-Tribonianus, chaps. 1–2, 7–9, 12–13 (1567); Conring, De origine iuris Germanici, chaps, 21–27, 32–34 (1641).

[25] Grotius, I, 1, 3.

[26] Suarez, De legibus ac deo legislatore, I, 8, § 1, I, 9, § 2; Soto, De justitia et jure, I, q. 5, a. 2.

[27] Grotius, I, 1, 9 § 1; Rutherforth, Institutes of Natural Law, I, 1, § 1 (1754).

[28] Burlamaqui, Principes du droit de la nature et des gens, I, chap. 5, § 10 and chap. 10, §§ 1–7; Wolff, Institutiones iuris naturae et gentium, §§ 74–102; Vattel, Le droit des gens, liv. I, chap. 2, §§ 15–17.

[29] Wilson, Lectures on Law, chaps. 2, 3.

[30] Traité de législation, I, 133 (1802).

[31] *Ibid.*

[32] *Ibid.*

[33] As to America, see Haines, The Revival of Natural Law Concepts (1930); Cohen, Law and the Social Order, 165–247 (1933). As to Europe: Leibholz, Les tendences actuelles du droit public en Allemagne, 1931, Archives de philosophie du droit et de sociologie juridique, 207–24; Hedemann, Die Flucht in die Generalklauseln (1933); Carlo, I diritto naturale nell' attuale fase del pensiero Italiano (1932); Pound, Fifty Years of Jurisprudence, 51 Harvard Law Rev. 444, 463–473.

[34] De iure belli ac pacis, prolegomena, §§ 15–16, bk. II, chap. II, 4, 5; bk. I, chap. I, 12.

[35] I have put this more at length in Interpretations of Legal History, 1–2.

[36] Radbruch, Rechtsphilosophie, 3 ed., 54–55 (1932);

Binder, Philosophie des Rechts, § 8 (1925); Pound, Twentieth Century Ideas as to the End of Law, Harvard Legal Essays, 357, 366–368 (1934); *id.* Fifty Years of Jurisprudence, 51 Harvard Law Rev. 444, 456–7, 461–3.

[37] Compare the dates in Odgers (and others) A Century of Law Reform with the dates of New York legislation, *supra*, note 1.

[38] Transition from a contractual theory of law to a historical theory is suggested in Blackstone's Commentaries. Blackstone conceives of the written law as consented to through representatives in Parliament (I Blackstone, Commentaries, 158–59), but of the unwritten law as made up of immemorial customs, that is, in effect as resting on historical bases (*id.* 63–73 — *cf.* the contract way of putting it, that the common law is a body of statutes worn down by time, in Hale, History of the Common Law, chap. 1). Whether the unwritten law is declaratory of natural law as he suggests in one passage, or is founded on a consent implied in the customary course of popular action, Blackstone does not decide (I Blackstone, Commentaries, 42). In James Wilson's Lectures (1790) the transition has gone further so that consent by a legal transaction is giving way to consent by a custom of popular action (1 Wilson's Works, Andrews' ed. 57). With Kent natural rights have a historical content and the theoretical basis is in transition from natural law to history (2 Kent, Commentaries, 1–11 — cf. the natural law way of putting it in Walker, Introduction to American Law, 23 [1837]). In Story's writings the transition is complete from a contract basis of rights and contract basis of government to a historical basis, confirmed by a constitution, which declares natural rights with a historical content (1 Story, Commentaries on the Constitution of the United States, bk. 2, chap. 3, especially §§ 340, 348, 356).

[39] Pufendorf, De jure naturae et gentium, cap. XIII; Rutherforth, Institutes of Natural Law, bk. I, chap. I, § 7

(1779 ed. 9–12); Burlamaqui, Principes du droit naturel, pt. I, chap. V, § 4; Vattel, Le droit des gens, preliminaires, 5.

[40] *E.g.* Wilson's Works, Andrews' ed. I, 57, 74.

[41] De jure belli ac pacis, I, I, 12.

[42] *Id.* prolegomena, § 30.

[43] "Eternal principles of justice which no government has a right to disregard." State Bank *v.* Cooper, 2 Yerger (Tenn.) 599, 603 (1831). See also Ham *v.* McClaws, 1 Bay (S. C.) 91, 98 (1789).

[44] Holden *v.* James, 11 Mass. 396, 398, 403–5 (1814); Chase, J. in Calder *v.* Bull, 3 Dall. (U. S.) 386, 388 (1798); Story, J. in Wilkinson *v.* Leland, 2 Pet. (U. S.) 627, 657 (1829).

[45] Walker, Introduction to American Law, §§ 11–12 (1837); Benson *v.* Mayer, 10 Barb. (N. Y.) 223, 244–45 (1850).

[46] Field, J., in Butcher's Union Co. *v.* Crescent City Co., 111 U. S. 746, 757 (1884). Compare the way in which the definition of direct and indirect taxation in John Stuart Mills' Political Economy became a part of Canadian constitutional law, Cotton *v.* The King, 15 D. L. R. 283, 290–92.

[47] Pound, The End of Law as Developed in Juristic Thought, 30 Harvard Law Rev. 201, 203–210; Sharswood, Legal Ethics, 5 ed., 22; Carter, Law: Its Origin, Growth and Function, 337; O'Brien, J., in People *v.* Coler, 166 N. Y. 1, 14–19.

[48] See his remarks on natural law, Complete Works, 1873 ed., I, 189, 197.

[49] The Civil Code of Georgia provided for by statute in 1858 and put into effect in 1860, the Field draft codes in New York, and to some extent the Negotiable Instruments law, the first of the Uniform State Laws under the auspices of the National Conference of Commissioners on Uniform State Laws, may serve as examples. See Carter, Law: Its Origin, Growth and Function, lects. XI, XII; Dillon, Laws

and Jurisprudence of England and America, 178–187; Hoadley, Annual Address before the American Bar Association, 11 Rep. Am. Bar Assn. 219 (1889); Ames, The Negotiable Instruments Law, 14 Harvard Law Rev. 442, supplementary note 15 Harvard Law Rev. 26.

[50] In section II of Blackstone's introduction (of the nature of laws in general) Pufendorf is cited four times and Grotius twice.

[51] Works of John Adams, II, 46.

[52] *Id.* 101, 103.

[53] Literary Diary of Ezra Stiles, III, 420.

[54] Van Santvoord, Lives of the Chief Justices of the United States (1 ed.) 6 n.

[55] Baldwin, The Study of Elementary Law, 13 Yale Law Journ. 1, 3.

[56] Kent, Memoirs of Chancellor Kent, 19.

[57] Private Correspondence of Daniel Webster (ed. by Fletcher Webster, 1857) 19.

[58] See Harvard University Annual Catalogue, 1849–50, p. 60.

[59] Gray, Nature and Sources of the Law, § 538, 2 ed., p. 253.

[60] *E.g.* Werner, J. in Ives *v.* South Buffalo R. Co., 201 N. Y. 271, 285–7, 293–5. Cf. Winslow, J., in Nunnemacher *v.* State, 129 Wis. 190, 199–202; Noel *v.* Ewing, 9 Ind. 37, 61; In re Moore's Estate, 114 Ore. 444; Smith *v.* Smith, 48 N. J. Eq. 566, 590.

[61] The most notable examples are the constitutions and bills of rights at the end of the eighteenth century. Legislative development of the law as to private corporations and as to homesteads and mechanics' liens on land may also be cited.

[62] Saleilles, L'individualisation de la peine, preface, ii.

[63] Jellinek, Allgemeine Staatslehre, 2 ed., 89 ff., 324 ff.

[64] Jurisprudence, 5 ed., 217.

II

LEGISLATION

GREAT things were expected of legislative lawmaking in the beginnings of our polity. Many looked forward to an American code which no less than our Constitution was to embody the idea upon our seal — *novus ordo saeclorum.*[1] It was not doubted that legislation would carry the chief burden of making an American law. Yet the results of our legislative reform movement fell far short of the anticipations with which it began. The latter part of the nineteenth century distrusted legislatures as profoundly as late eighteenth-century America distrusted executives.[2] In the end judicial decision rather than legislation proved to have pulled the laboring oar and even doctrinal writing, of which the common-law tradition had no great opinion, proved to have furnished most of the power behind the courts.

American legislation began with every advantage. Despite our constitutional theory of three co-ordinate and co-equal departments of government, the hegemony of the legislative department from the beginning to the time of the Civil War is clear enough. Legislators thought of themselves as peculiarly the representatives of the sovereign people, with all the powers of the sovereign devolved upon them. As late as the impeachment of Andrew Johnson it was confidently asserted that the executive was accountable to the legislative for the exercise of powers committed to the executive by the Constitution.[3] All through the formative era legislative assemblies assumed that courts were accountable to them for the way in which they decided controversies. State legislatures summoned judges before them to be interrogated as to particular decisions exactly after the manner of the famous colloquy between James I and the judges of England.[4] There was an idea of legislative omnicompetence. The earlier legislatures did not hesitate to enact statutes reversing judgments of the courts in particular cases.[5] They sought to admit to probate wills rejected by the courts.[6] They sought to dictate the details of administration of particular estates.[7] By special laws they directed the details of local government for particular instances. They validated particular invalid marriages.[8] They suspended the statute of limitations for a particular litigant in a particular case.[9] They exempted a particular wrongdoer from liability for a particular wrong for which his neighbors would be held by the general law.[10]

What was behind the extravagant faith in legislative assemblies to which such phenomena testify? Politically it grows out of the conditions of a time in which the absolute governments characteristic of the seventeenth and eighteenth centuries were giving way before a rising tide of democracy. It is reinforced by the victory of Parliament in the contests of Parliament with the Crown which culminated in the English Revolution of 1688, and by the part taken by the assembly in the French Revolution. On its legal side many things contributed. Statesmen and lawyers of the time were deeply read in French and Dutch publicists who thought of the Roman law as a body of legislation, as it had been taught since the Middle Ages. The common law, as something English, was under a cloud after our Revolution. Roman law was taken to be embodied reason and historical scholars had not made men aware that behind the legislative form of that law was a long development of juristic opinions on detailed points in concrete cases very analogous to the development of English law by judicial decision. The Byzantine-Roman conception of law as the will of an absolute lawgiver pervaded the law books of the Continent. Then, too, there was the idea of the lawmaker producing merely by an effort of reason a complete code, which community and judges might take as ultimate wisdom; an idea which was propagated by the law-of-nature school. There was the Rousseauist idea of law as the "expression of the general will" with the legislature as the organ of that will, and a generation of legislators drawing conclusions from the phrase "representatives of the people." There was the example of the Codes, French, Prussian, and Austrian, which sprang up at the end of the eighteenth and the beginning of the nineteenth century. There was a certain momentum left over from the lawmaking urge of the Puritan Revolution which had led to a flood of lawmaking in more than one of the colonies where the Puritans were strong.[11] There was the doctrine of separation of powers which, taken literally as late as 1915, led to a proposal in the New York Constitutional Convention of that year to forbid anything more than a mechanical judicial application of established rules.[12]

Most of all, however, the legislative was the first of our departments of government to get its growth. It was the first to develop in the colonies and it took on an American aspect from the start. Prior to the Revolution the executive was a royal governor or proprietary governor and so could afford no model for the future. In the first century of colonial existence courts were not needed on any large scale. Magistrates, with an appeal to the legislature or to some council or to the executive, sufficed for the simpler relations of the beginnings. Legislatures on the model of the representative lower house of Parliament were set up generally from an early time and by the eighteenth century had attained strength and had obtained the confidence of the public. The English polity after 1688 made men familiar with a sovereign legislature as, in the two centuries before, Tudors and Stuarts and the old regime in France had made them familiar with a sovereign king. In more than one of our states until well after the Revolution, legislatures claimed and exercised the plenary powers over adjudication and administration which belonged to the British Parliament.

What did legislation achieve for American law in the height of legislative leadership from the Revolution to the Civil War? When we compare the permanent results with those of judicial decision in the same period and reflect on the volume of local statute making, we must admit it did relatively little. The enduring creative legislation of the time is almost entirely in constitutions and bills of rights, federal and state. Certainly legislation gave our common-law jurisdictions nothing in private law of such significance as the Code Napoléon or as your Civil Code here in Louisiana.

For the most part it did away with survivals in seventeenth-century English law which had not been eliminated in the wake of the Puritan Revolution, and for the rest formulated what jurists of the school of natural law and courts of equity had worked out and made ready for legislative adoption. One can number on his fingers the outstanding statutes of the era which have an enduring place in our private law. In truth, the legislative reform movement, especially in England, was chiefly taken up with repeal. It abrogated rules and institutions which had come down from feudal England. It pruned away restrictions on free individual activity which spoke from the relationally organized society of the Middle Ages and had ceased to be applicable to a society organized on the basis of free individual competitive self-assertion. What it reshaped, as for example in the Married Women's Acts, was mostly reshaped to the patterns laid out by equity.

Undoubtedly the best work of our nineteenth-century legislation was done in criminal law and penal administration. Natural law had little scope in judicial finding of law on the criminal side. The general security calls for more rule and less latitude of application here than anywhere else unless in the law of estates in land. There was little place here for creative judicial decision such as that of Lord Mansfield on quasi contract and on the law merchant. Critical natural law found one of its best fields in penal legislation and administration. But there was little scope for judicial development of that subject. What has been done for American penal administration, what has been done for American criminal law, has been mostly legislative. Except for one writer of the first magnitude at the very end of the formative era, doctrinal writers have neglected it, and law schools, which have done so much for the law in every other connection, have left this branch to take care of itself.[13] Even if the field had been suited to judicial creative work, judicial decision lacked at this point the help which has made it effective in other connections. Here was *par excellence* the opportunity of legislation. Is it not significant that while notable strides have been made in every other department of law, our criminal law has been and remains relatively stagnant?

It would seem that while legislation has proved an effective agency of ridding the law of particular institutions and precepts which have come down from the past and have not been adapted or were not adaptable to the needs of the time, it has not been able, in our legal system, except in rare instances, to do much of the constructive work of change in eras of growth. So far as everyday relations and conflicts of interests are concerned, it has not been able to anticipate new demands nor to move fast enough when they made themselves felt through litigation. Judicial finding of law has a real advantage in competition with legislation in that it works with concrete cases and generalizes only after a long course of trial and error in the effort to work out a practicable principle. Legislation, when more than declaratory, when it does more than restate authoritatively what judicial experience has indicated, involves the difficulties and the perils of prophecy. But these considerations are not enough, of themselves, to explain why we, in common-law America, in comparison with the civil-law world, have been able to do so little in the way of enduring monuments of legislative law-making.

What are the reasons for the relative failure of American legislation of the formative era to do what was expected of it? Certainly it was not that the English-speaking world lacked leaders for legislative lawmaking. Three names among those who urged and sought to guide legislation in common-law jurisdictions are at least as great as any among contemporary judges or doctrinal writers. Put in chronological order, they are: Jeremy Bentham (1743–1832),[14] Edward Livingston (1764–1836),[15] and David Dudley Field (1805–1894).[16]

Each of these exceptionally gifted men labored long and devotedly to give to the English-speaking legal world the best possible legislative law-making. But they could not legislate directly, whereas lesser men on the bench could hand down directly legal propositions of which other judges and doctrinal writers were bound to take account. Men of lesser stature could, in the role of doctrinal writers, direct the course of judicial decision much more than these masters of the science of legislation could direct the action of parliamentary law-makers. Thus more and more the growing point of our law came to be in judicial decision.

We can hardly say that legislative development of our law was hindered by the necessity of fitting legislation into the common law, which was traditionally unsympathetic to statutes. For it might well have happened, and an intelligent observer in the first quarter of a century after the Revolution might well have predicted, that the common law would have to fit into or adjust itself to a body of legislation. But one can see why, as the bench came to be manned by trained lawyers and their training came to be in the common-law tradition, the scope for effective legislation was sure to narrow. For one thing, the common law has never been at its best in administering justice from written texts. It has an excellent technique of finding the grounds of decision of particular cases in reported experience of the decision of other cases in the past. It has always, in comparison with the civil law, been awkward and none too effective in deciding on the basis of legislative texts. Moreover, its traditional attitude toward statutes stands in the way of making them a basis of creative development. The common law thinks of a statute as giving a rule, prescribing a detailed consequence for a detailed situation of fact, but not as a starting point for legal reasoning. While the civil law thinks of the course of judicial decision as providing a rule and turns for analogies to code or statute book, the common-law lawyer finds a rule in a statutory provision and takes his analogies from judicial decision. Nor does it stop here. He assumes that the statute is not meant to change the common law, or at least is meant to change it as little as possible, and so is prone to hold it declaratory if he can and at any rate to construe it strictly when it seeks to effect a change.[17] He thinks of the constitutional checks upon legislation as enacting common-law limitations, and systematically develops those checks in terms of the common law.[18] Thus the area of legislative reform of the law is restricted at the same time that effectiveness within the narrowed area is diminished.

How the common-law tradition operates when

a great piece of legislation is in the making is illustrated by the Sherman Anti-Trust Law. As John Sherman drew it originally it was a typical bit of Anglo-American legislation dealing specifically with a specific situation by a simple detailed rule. It provided, as he drew it, that in case of products of combinations in restraint of trade, the products of foreign competitors should come into the country free of duty. The judiciary committee of the Senate felt that this was not enough. They wished to draw a general statute as to such combinations. But they did not undertake to frame such a statute beyond a skeleton which they expected would be filled out by judicial decision. Senator Hoar tells us that they took it that by using the words of the common law they insured that the courts would take the act as a warrant for a gradual development of the common law on the subject. Instead of this, he tells us, the Supreme Court of the United States construed the words, not as at common law, but as meant to introduce a new rule, and so the statute was made to introduce a sweeping change.[19] One cannot put the whole blame of such things upon either legislature or courts. They are the result of an attitude which has a long-taught tradition behind it and will not readily yield. But they make the path of the legislative lawmaker a rough one.

We must remember, however, that the legislators of the formative era were full of confidence. They were in no wise held back by considerations of how statutes would be received and applied by the courts, and if they had retained the confidence of the public they might have forced a better judicial attitude. Instead they gradually lost it and the courts gradually acquired it, so that in the period from the Civil War to the end of the century the hegemony of the judiciary in our polity is as marked as was that of the legislature in the earlier period. There were many reasons for this growing distrust of legislatures which became strong in the last quarter of the nineteenth century, and we must look into them in some detail for the light they throw upon the question what we may expect to achieve through legislation in another era of legal growth.

In part the very enthusiasm for legislation that came in the wake of the French Revolution could but bring about a reaction. From the first there was a strong reaction from the paper constitution making and institutional waste as they went on across the water, and as Europe settled down to an era of what has been called bourgeois liberalism after 1848, so the followers of Jefferson and Jackson showed a growing conservatism toward the middle of the century. Then, too, historical thinking came to be in the air. Burke had insisted on historical continuity and Savigny had founded a historical school of jurists which was skeptical as to legislation and opposed to codes. The doctrine of this school spread slowly to America. But it was taught at Harvard by a pupil of Savigny from 1848 to 1851.[20] As the momentum of the legislative reform movement was spent, American lawyers ceased to believe that creative legislation was possible; or at least came to believe it not possible beyond authoritative formulation of rules which got their content from custom of popular action or judicial experience.[21] Along with this rise of historical thinking went a waning of natural law. By the end of the third quarter of the century the courts were repudiating it as decisively as they had confidently announced it fifty years before.[22] The growth of academic law schools and an academically trained profession steeped in the common-law tradition put the last touches to the change.

Livingston did not found a school of jurists to carry on his ideas to their undoing. But Bentham's ideas underwent a transformation in the hands of his followers as the English legislative reform movement became spent also. This grew out of certain intrinsic difficulties in Bentham's doctrine. It had a negative as well as a positive side and his creative idea of utility could be, and it was, used only to remove archaisms rather than to build anew. Bentham sought to free his generation from the shackles upon free action which had come down from the relationally organized society of the Middle Ages. He agreed entirely with the metaphysical and historical jurists on the Continent that the law should bring about a maximum of free individual self-assertion by taking off restraints rather than imposing them.[23] His followers had as little belief in the social legislation that was in the near future as had the followers of Savigny or, later, Herbert Spencer.[24] It was not a time for creative legislation. For a season the task was one of organizing and systematizing the results of a past period of growth. Accordingly, Bentham's followers of the last third of the century developed a juristic pessimism substantially identical with that of Savigny's school. They said we could not add to or produce human happiness by legislation; we could only remove hindrances to men's finding happiness for themselves.[25]

With the development of the legal profession, the growth of confidence in the judiciary and the rise of academic legal education based on the common law, a contest between courts and legislatures began in our formative era which is comparable to the contests between courts and crown in seventeenth-century England and was in part brought about, so far as the courts are concerned, by the influence of the legal literature of the English contest, which was classical for the lawyer.

In seventeenth-century England the courts had stood for the common-law doctrine that no official action was above the law as against arbitrary rulers in an age of absolute governments. In nineteenth-century America certain grave abuses of legislation led the judges in the states to insist upon constitutional checks designed to meet those abuses and to stand for the common-law doctrine of the supremacy of the law as a doctrine that the legislature itself is subject to the Constitution as the supreme law of the land, to be interpreted and applied by the courts in the course of orderly litigation as in any other case involving finding and application of law.

One of these abuses, against which state constitutions provided every sort of drastic limitation, was involved in special legislation. The American legislator found his warrant for this type of law-making in Blackstone. The latter distinguishes general or public from special or private acts. He says:

"The statute 13 Eliz. c. 10, to prevent spiritual persons from making leases for longer terms than three lives or twenty-one years is a public act, it being a rule prescribed to the whole body of spiritual persons in the nation; but an act to enable the Bishop of Chester to make a lease to A. B. for sixty years is an exception to this rule; it concerns only the parties and the bishop's successors and is, therefore, a private act." [26]

Special legislation of this sort is legislative administration rather than legislative lawmaking. It could have raised nice questions as to the constitutional separation of powers. But the volume of it and abuses to which it gave rise, for we can scarcely credit, as we know state legislation today, what the session laws of an older time disclose, led to provisions in state constitutions prohibiting it or limiting it, either generally or to certain subjects or classes of subjects. These provisions were often difficult to interpret and to apply and were not always easy for lawmakers to adhere to. They gave rise to much litigation and in more than one state involved important statutes in uncertainty session after session. This condition did not make for good legislation.[27]

No less abuses grew up with respect to amending and supplementing legislation. Amendments were superposed on previous legislation without being fitted in where they belonged or with any consideration of where they belonged in an intelligible statute book or how they should be fitted into it. They gave rise to doubts as to where to put them in the body of statute law and led to questions as to implied repeals, creating doubts whether anything was intended to be or had been repealed and if so how much and exactly what. Not so long ago the English statute books were in a scandalous condition in this respect. So also were our federal statutes till recently. Nineteenth-century state constitutions sought to deal with these abuses by strict requirements as to how laws should be revived or amended or repealed. These provisions also were hard to comply with and hard to interpret and apply. In many states they gave the courts much trouble and led to almost as much uncertainty as to what was statute law as the abuses to which they were directed.[28]

Grave abuses grew up also with respect to riders on bills whereby surreptitious clauses were introduced as to which the public had little or no chance of making itself heard in opposition. Hence many state constitutions made strict provisions as to the title of acts and correspondence of the content with the title, or as to the number of subjects which could be included in one act, which involved quite as much confusion in application and had quite as unhappy effects upon statute lawmaking as in the cases of special legislation, amendment, and repeal.[29]

Along with the foregoing abuses there was a

tendency of legislatures to interfere with executive administration and with exercise of the judicial function. There were legislative prescribings of appointment of particular persons to particular offices by the governor.[30] There was special legislation as to local highway improvements where today we should leave the matter to a board or commission. There were legislative prescribings as to admission to the bar, even as to the admission of a particular person or reinstatement of a particular disbarred lawyer.[31] There were legislative prescribings that judges should do the work of law reporting by writing judicial head notes to opinions.[32] Here difficult questions were raised as to the constitutional distribution or separation of powers. Such things go far to explain the persistence in the United States of the common-law attitude toward statutes which is admittedly an unhappy feature of our Anglo-American legal tradition. Instead of legislatures and courts working together toward the ends of law, in the last century, if they were not actually in conflict, they tended each to be suspicious of the other. Partly this was an inheritance from the seventeenth-century English polity upon which ours was built. Partly it was involved in the application to legislation of our common-law doctrine of the supremacy of the law. Partly it is a phase of the general regime of non-co-operation, of independent agencies of government pursuing their individual ways independently, which was characteristic of pioneer America on every side.[33] It became more marked in the second half of the century as the personnel of state lawmaking bodies declined.

In many cases in the first third of the nineteenth century state courts took Blackstone's statement that "no human laws are of any validity" if contrary to the law of nature as a warrant for refusing to apply statutes which they considered arbitrary and unreasonable. Thus in 1822 the Supreme Court of Connecticut said that if a statute without any cause deprived a person of his property or subjected him to imprisonment, so that there was a "direct infraction of vested rights too palpable to be questioned and too unjust to admit of vindication," it would be "a violation of the social compact and within the control of the judiciary."[34] In 1814, in passing on an act which dispensed with the provisions of the statute of limitations in favor of a particular creditor as against a particular debtor, the Supreme Court of Massachusetts said:

"It is manifestly against the first principles of civil liberty and natural justice and the spirit of our constitution and laws that any one citizen should enjoy privileges and advantages which are denied to all others under like circumstances, or that any one should be subjected to losses, damages, suits or actions from which all others under like circumstances are exempted." [35]

Likewise in 1831 the Supreme Court of Tennessee said that since there are "eternal principles of justice which no government has a right to disregard," it did not follow that "because there may be no restriction in the Constitution prohibiting a particular act of the legislature that such act is therefore constitutional." It added: "Some acts, although not expressly forbidden, may be against the plain and obvious dictates of reason." Accordingly the court refused to give effect to a retroactive statute creating a special tribunal to try certain suits by a bank against its officers.[36]

Since the Fourteenth Amendment such statutes come within the express prohibition of the Constitution. But in our formative era there was no other check than the common-law tradition from the Middle Ages that all official action was subject to the law and was not to be arbitrary and unreasonable. This doctrine had been applied by Coke in 1610 in Bonham's Case,[37] and by Hobart in 1615 in Day *v.* Savadge,[38] and Holt had laid down in 1701, in City of London *v.* Wood,[39] that an act of Parliament "cannot make one that lives under a government judge and party." Under the influence of the idea of popular omnicompetence and hence of legislative absolutism in the representatives of the people, and of laws as formulations of the popular will, reinforced later by ideas of law as the command of the sovereign, there was a marked tendency to arbitrariness in legislation. The memory of contests between courts and crown over the royal dispensing power was too recent to lead common-law courts to admit a like arbitrary legislative dispensing power. The taught tradition was averse to absolute power anywhere.[40] That was what constitutions and bills of rights sought to preclude, and things which colonial legislatures had done were among the mischiefs which our constitutional separation of powers was designed to obviate. But all power is liable to abuse and power must exist somewhere if a politically organized society is to do its work. That the line which the courts took in the end has been followed and found practicable for a century speaks for itself. On the whole the courts worked out a difficult balance well in our formative era. If natural law led to some extravagances for a time, its rationalism proved a useful guide.

Perhaps legislatures are more unmindful than courts of the limitations of effective legal action. They have to predict detailed applications where the court draws its principle from detailed applications after the event and in the light of experienced limitations. But well as judicial scrutiny of legislative action has worked, looked at as a whole, it must be admitted to have had a bad effect in lessening the sense of legislative responsibility. Observers have often remarked a tendency, in common phrase, to pass the buck to the courts, comparable to the tendency to leave it to the courts, or today to administrative agencies, to fill out a skeleton statute. Part of the relative ineffectiveness of state legislatures in matters of law reform must be attributed to this irresponsibility.

We may understand what led the courts of our formative era into the attitude toward legislation which prevailed in the nineteenth century and yet deprecate continuance of the traditional suspicion of statutes into the present time. The historical thinking of the immediate past suspected statutes because they were likely to involve breaches of continuity. Also the Benthamite and Kantian and Positivist thinking of nineteenth-century jurists looked askance at them because as the pressure of new interests led to what we have called social legislation, statutes tended to infringe the conception of law as a regime of hands off in which the only justification of a particular legal restraint was that it tended to promote an abstract general freedom. These modes of thought aggravated the tendency of courts to ignore important legislation by deciding it to be declaratory or even by assuming silently that it was declaratory, adducing no reasons and simply citing the decisions of the past. They led the lawyers of the last generation to harp overmuch on the deficiencies of legislation at a time when the mechanism of legislative lawmaking was fast improving. They led to a fashion of preaching too dogmatically the inevitable superiority of judicially found law.

Modern statutes are not to be disposed of so lightly as offhand products of a vaguely conceived desire to do something. Not infrequently they represent long and patient study by experts, careful consideration by conferences or congresses or associations, discussions in periodicals or in the press, in which public opinion is directed upon important details, and long and intelligently conducted hearings before legislative committees. Moreover, judicial finding of law in the last century was not without its faults. The jurisprudence of conceptions led for a time to an overmechanical development in which attempt was made to reduce all law to an aggregate of rules on the model of rules of property. The received judicial and professional ideal of the legal order as a regime of maintaining a maximum of free individual self-assertion led to judicial attempts, particularly in the state courts, to force Benthamite ideas of freedom of contract and Spencerian ideas of individualism into the standard of due process of law. The presumption that statutes are declaratory or at least that they do not derogate from the common law led courts to retard the efficacy of uniform state laws on commercial subjects.[41]

One difficulty, then, with which legislation has had to contend, and, indeed, still has to contend in the United States, is a feeling on the part of lawyers and courts that anything beyond some change of some detailed rule, based on judicial experience of the working of that rule and formulating the result, is out of place in the legal system; that it is an alien element to be held down strictly and not to be applied beyond its express language. This settled feeling is expressed in a doctrine that statutes in derogation of the common law are to be strictly construed — a doctrine which has persisted in the face of a century of legislative attempts to abrogate it [42] — and in the settled technique of our law which finds analogies only in the common law and refuses to take a statutory provision as a starting point for legal reasoning. We do not receive a statute fully into the body of the law, on a complete equality with judicially found precepts, so that like the latter the statutory precepts give both rules and principles to be developed by analogy. Hence new policies behind modern legislation fare hardly for a time until they are taken up gradually through judicial decision. This, however, is not at all a purely American phenomenon. We inherited it from England and today it is quite as much English as American. How thoroughly it is part of the Anglo-American legal tradition is illustrated in a note in the twelfth edition of Holland's Jurisprudence (1916). Holland was by creed an analytical jurist and as such, in other connections, took a statute for the type of a law. But he was so trained in the common-law tradition that when his eye fell upon an article which I wrote in the Harvard Law Review in 1908, showing the history and reasons back of that tradition and challenging its applicability to the social legislation of this century, he was impelled to add a note as to "legislation and adjudication as instruments for bringing law into harmony with social progress" and add that "till parliamentary draftsmanship and procedure are vastly improved, the preference will hardly be given to legislation." [43]

Yet we must not overlook intrinsic difficulties in legislative lawmaking under popular government. There is a sound element in Savigny's doctrine. Mr. Justice Holmes tells us that historical continuity in law is not a duty, it is a necessity.[44] If lawyers too often insist upon the duty, legislators quite as often overlook the necessity. Our state statute books are full of statutes which are no more than survivals from a time when they had some vitality. Too many of them were not enforceable from the beginning. It is quite as possible for recent legislation as for past decision to be out of touch with the time. It does not follow that there is no such thing as creative legislative lawmaking. It is true enough that nothing in law is made entirely out of whole cloth. The historical jurist of the last century was right in insisting that legislature or doctrinal writer put in the form of legal precepts what had already been worked out in experience. But the law-of-nature school were not wholly in error when they saw a finding of the just precept by reason and an authoritative formulation of it by the lawmaker. What we mean when we speak of creative legislation is legislation which brings new principles or starting points for legal reasoning into the law from without instead of merely formulating authoritatively what has come in already in another way through juristic writing or judicial decision. The Workmen's Compensation Acts are an example. But such legislation is not common. If Savigny does not give us an ultimate dogma, he gives us a much needed caution.

It should be added that caution as to legislative lawmaking is the more to be expected in the Anglo-

American lawyer. For his is a frame of mind which prefers to go forward step by step on the basis of experience from this case or that case to the next case, as justice in each case seems to require, instead of seeking to refer everything back to or deduce it from supposed universals. It is the frame of mind behind what is sometimes referred to as the Anglo-Saxon habit of muddling through, which is really a habit of dealing with things as they arise instead of seeking over-ambitiously to anticipate them by universal formulas. Recent juristic writing on the Continent indicates that this concrete mode of thought is making its way among the civilians also.

As the world is organized politically today, or at least as the Western World was organized until the recent coming of dictators, legislation means parliamentary lawmaking. But the great monuments of legislation on legal, as distinguished from political subjects, have not come from popularly elected assemblies. We cannot overlook that such assemblies have not been too likely to choose the most expert advisers or reporters to draft laws, that the formulating process which goes before their action has involved grave defects, that politics may play an unhappy role where it should be excluded, that there has been legislative carelessness far beyond anything exhibited in judicial decision, and that the system of informing the legislative lawmaker upon the matters as to which he is to legislate is usually crude and inadequate. Such draftsmen as Livingston and Field had little success in getting their most mature work adopted, and while the Swiss had the good sense to employ the learning and skill of Huber, most of the significant codes have not proceeded from democratic assemblies.

Even more, legislation by legislative assemblies suffers from the process of preparation in which politics necessarily plays a great part. Important public agencies of preparation have grown up in the present century and are achieving good results. But in the formative era the work devolved almost entirely upon legislative committees and so lacked continuity and system and was done unevenly and at random in the hurry of a busy session. Soon the field was taken over by private agencies, which came to exercise a controlling influence. Chief among these was a type of organization representing some particular interest and advocating measures drawn up solely with an eye to the demands of that interest. Today every trade, every business, every industry, every profession has its organization and its legislative committee. Every such organization has its biennial or even annual budget of bills. Each for the most part succeeds in procuring the legislation which it urges. As a rule it fails only when the laws demanded are opposed by some other organization no less powerful and no less persistent. Take, for example, federal legislation as to interpleader. That useful proceeding had come to be encumbered by technical limitations, historical in origin, which greatly hampered its usefulness. A few years ago it became the subject of federal legislation, governing the federal courts. That legislation extended the scope of the proceeding and did away with the historical technical limitations in the case of insurance companies, surety companies and fraternal insurance organizations.[45] For the rest, litigants in the federal courts were left where they were before the statute. The insurance companies and surety companies were organized and could urge the remedial act. It was no one's business to study the whole subject of interpleader and draft and promote legislation putting it on a modern basis. It has taken the public-spirited voluntary activity of a law teacher to better this bad situation.[46]

Then, too, a legislative assembly today has to get through an enormous amount of work in a limited time. Political matters, appropriations, the machinery of government, provisions for administration and police, must have the right of way. Even now after great improvements have been made in the way of legislative counsel, legislative councils, and drafting bureaus, the necessary rush of a busy session involves much carelessness in statute lawmaking. There are no such checks upon legislative carelessness as those which compel courts to proceed cautiously with an assurance that at any rate they know what they are doing and on what basis.

Most of all, however, American legislation has suffered from an undeveloped technique as compared with our developed judicial technique. We inherited no legislative technique and the simpler conditions of our earlier lawmaking did not seem to call for it. But the reports are full of illustrations of what this want of technique could bring about. Interpretation clauses and statutory definitions came to be resorted to, partly to assure that the statute would be understood, partly in order to constrain judicial action in the contests between courts and legislatures. But there are many reported cases where these clauses and definitions have served only to darken counsel.[47] There is more than one case in the books where the context and apparent purpose of the act have indicated one thing and the interpretation clause another.[48] In many cases the use of vague and general terms has raised difficult questions as to how far courts could resort to judicial legislation to give an act some concrete content.[49] There have been many cases in which there was nothing in the way of context or other laws *in pari materia* by which to eke out a statute where the provisions were so obscure that a court, with best of intention, could not ascertain and declare its proper meaning.[50] Such things have led to popular agitation for spurious interpretation, sometimes by the very persons who in other connections have inveighed against what they called judicial usurpation. This was well marked at the beginning of the present century. Much of which there was complaint was due quite as much to legislative crudity as to judicial narrowness. For down even to the present, courts have had continually to deal with such things as failure to provide any machinery for carrying out statutory provisions;[51] as use of a name or term which seems free from doubt on its face without learning or appreciating the cases or circumstances to which it must apply, so that the name or term is hopelessly ambiguous when applied to the facts;[52] as making a general provision requiring a certain fixing of details and omitting any provision for those details;[53] or as using such vague terms that they cannot be applied to any actual conditions.[54]

On many occasions I have urged a ministry of justice both for the nation and in each state as the remedy for such things.[56] For the time has gone by when the only research needed for improvement of the law was study of law books and law reports aided by the experience of the lawmaker or judge and the general knowledge of his neighbors. In the past the social and economic background of the making and application of legal precepts required little study. Mostly it was patent to the observation of an intelligent man without special training or special effort. Today we cannot assume that lawmaker, law finder and law enforcer may discover in the texts and in their own experience of life or general knowledge of men and things all that is needed for a due functioning of the legal order. The problems are no longer obvious, nor are the applications to them of the historical materials, when once discovered, or the needed adaptation of the legal machinery to them, when once defined, any more obvious. We cannot much longer rely upon spontaneous individual effort, especially as it usually means the pressure of the individual demands of some interested group or organization.

What, then, may we expect from legislative lawmaking in the creative era of legal growth which is at hand? Thirty years ago, when the state courts seemed slow to appreciate the problems raised by the legislation of the time and were for the most part still trying to reduce the whole administration of justice to mechanical application of rules of the type of rules of property, I suggested that judicial decision as an agency of legal growth bade fair to become sterile, that we must look forward to a shifting of the growing point of our law to legislation, and that we needed to recast our ideas of the relation of the traditional law to legislation and learn from the civilian to use modern statutes as declaratory of general policies and so as starting points for creative legal reasoning.[56] But having to teach a course in legislation for two years recently, I was required to study the statute books of the last century and to go through the reports to study the questions raised upon them and decided by the courts. This study convinced me that the matter was by no means so simple as I had assumed. I still feel strongly as I did then that the common-law lawyer must learn a different attitude toward statutes. But there is very much more to be done. Judicial decision is showing a revived creative power while legislatures are turning creative work over to administrative boards and commissions and tribunals. Much has been done in the present generation to improve legislative technique, but much more than good technique is needed if statutes are to do what we demand of them. We cannot expect to get on without legislation. It is the characteristic mode of lawmaking in matured systems.

It is futile to expect that the preliminary work of searching for, organizing, and making available the data required for lawmaking, judicial law finding, and administrative enforcement will do itself. Nor may it be done by the old machinery of legislative committees working under pressure at the crisis of lawmaking, of courts deciding controversies on local fragments of national questions under limitations of jurisdiction, venue and parties, and of administrative tribunals treating every case as unique. Even more it is futile to expect sound results from research done to order for some special interest or done in a commercial or partisan spirit.

But we are not concerned at the moment with preparation for adjudication or administrative determination. At any rate, so far as the law governing the everyday relations of man and man is concerned, our process of legislative lawmaking will not suffice. As it goes on and has gone on for a generation, it detracts from the effectiveness of law and injures respect for law. Whatever may be their value for great social and political questions, legislative hearings and inquiries, as now conducted, are as inadequate for the improvement of the authoritative materials of judicial decision as the much criticized modes of stimulating judicial notice of social conditions and economic realities. It is imperative to develop competent, scientific, impartial agencies of preparation. It is not enough to urge a change of heart upon courts and lawyers. We must direct our attention to the agencies of statute lawmaking, to the materials upon which those agencies must work, to the auxiliary apparatus which they can command, and to ways of improving those materials, organizing that apparatus, and making the agencies and the apparatus more effective for their purpose.

[1] See Walker, Introduction to American Law, 58–61, 648–9 (1837).

[2] Bryce, The American Commonwealth, I, 427–8, 451–2.

[3] Trial of Andrew Johnson, III, 131, 215, 248–253.

[4] Prohibitions del Roy, 12 Rep. 63. Legislative calling of judges to account for decisions: Trevett *v.* Weeden, 2 Chandler, Criminal Trials, 269 (1786); Doolan, The Old Court–New Court Controversy, 11 Green Bag, 177; Blair *v.* Williams, 4 Litt. (Ky.) 34; Statutes 2 T. B. Mon. (Ky.) iii–xvi, 3 *id.* i–ii; Lynch, The Bench and Bar of Mississippi, 92–97; Somerville, A Sketch of the Supreme Court of Mississippi, 503, 505–6.

[5] Preface, 1 Chipman (Vt.) 21 ff.; Merrill *v.* Sherburne, 1 N. H. 199; Calder *v.* Bull, 2 Root (Conn.) 350; Hamilton *v.* Hemsted, 3 Day (Conn.) 338; Calder *v.* Bull, 3 Dall. (U. S.) 386; Plumer, Life of William Plumer, 170. "Frequently during the first half of the century the legislature interfered to direct specific cases to be heard at the first term after arrival of the cases [instead of standing over to a later term according to the regular practice], and in at least one instance, such a provision was made by legislative enactment

for a case not yet disposed of in the trial jurisdiction. And legislation was passed ordering proceedings to be taken in particular cases, for instance, ordering dismissed cases to be reinstated." Bond, The Court of Appeals of Maryland, 133, citing a succession of statutes from 1837 to 1880.

[6] Calder *v.* Bull, 3 Dall (U. S.) 386.

[7] Leland *v.* Wilkinson, 6 Pet. (U. S.) 317, 319.

[8] Local Laws of Indiana, 1842, chap. 140, p. 130.

[9] Holden *v.* James, 11 Mass. 396. Cf. Wheeler's Appeal, 45 Conn. 306; Ogden *v.* Blackledge, 2 Cranch (U. S.) 272. In Indiana there was frequent legislation dispensing for the benefit of particular specified litigants with the statutory requirements for bringing suit for divorce: Local Laws of Indiana, 1841, chap. 38, p. 40; Local Laws of Indiana, 1842, chap. 122, p. 119; *id.* chap. 125, p. 121.

[10] Holden *v.* James, *supra,* 405; Local Laws of Indiana, 1839, ch. 75, p. 158; Local Laws of Indiana, 1829, chap. 49, p. 97. See also Greenough *v.* Greenough, 11 Pa. St. 489, 494–6; Norman *v.* Heist, 5 Watts and Serg. (Pa.) 171.

[11] *E.g.* The Book of the General Laws and Liberties Concerning the Inhabitants of the Massachusetts [Legislative Compilation and revision of legislation chiefly from 1641 to 1647], reprinted from the 1648 edition, 1929; The Book of the General Laws for the People within the Jurisdiction of Connecticut, 1673; The Proceedings of the First General Assembly of the Incorporation of Providence Plantations and the Code of Laws adopted by that Assembly in 1647, ed. by Staples, 1847.

[12] 1 Revised Record of the Constitutional Convention of the State of New York (1915), 411. The substance of this may be found in Clarke, What May be Done to Enable the Courts to Allay the Present Discontent with the Administration of Justice, 50 American Law Rev. 161.

[13] Pound, Toward a Better Criminal Law, 60 Rep. Am. Bar Assn., 322.

[14] On Bentham see: Albee, History of English Utilitarianism; Allen, The Young Bentham, 44 Law Quarterly Rev. 492; Alexander, Bentham: Philosopher and Reformer, 7 New York Univ. Law Rev. 141, 405; Atkinson, Jeremy Bentham, His Life and Work; Berolzheimer, The World's Legal Philosophies, 134–141; Cohen, Jeremy Bentham (Fabian Tracts, no. 221); Dicey, Lectures on the Relation between Law and Public Opinion in England in the Nineteenth Century, lect. 6; Dillon, Laws and Jurisprudence of England and America, lect. 12, reprinted (revised) as "Bentham's Influence in the Reforms of the Nineteenth Century," 1 Select Essays in Anglo-American Legal History, 492; Everett, The Education of Jeremy Bentham; Geiser and Jaszi, Political Philosophy from Plato to Bentham, ch. 13; Greaves, Bentham on Legislative Procedure, Economica, no. 33, 308; Gregory, Bentham and the Codifiers, 13 Harvard Law Rev. 341; Halévy, La formation du radicalisme philosophique (English transl. by Morris, as The Growth of Philosophic Radicalism) contains also a full bibliography of Bentham's writings and of accounts of Bentham and estimates of his work; Judson, Modern View of the Law Reforms of Jeremy Bentham, 10 Columbia Law Rev. 41; Kayser, The Grand Social Enterprise: A Study of Jeremy Bentham in His Relation to Liberal Nationalism; Lundin, The Influence of Jeremy Bentham on English Democratic Development, 7 Iowa University Studies in Social Science, no. 3; MacCann, Bentham and His Philosophy of Reform; Mitchell, Bentham and His School, 35 Juridical Review, 248; Mitchell, Bentham's Felicific Calculus, 33 Political Science Quarterly, 161; Ogden, Introduction (in his ed. of Bentham's Theory of Legislation); Ogden, Bentham's Theory of Fictions; Phillipson, Three Criminal Law Reformers, pt. II, Bentham; Rockow, Bentham on the Theory of the Second Chamber, 22 American Political Science Review, 586; Stephen, The English Utilitarians, vol. I; Solari, L'idea individuale e

l'idea sociale nel diritto privato, §§ 31–36; Wallas, Jeremy Bentham; Wallas, Jeremy Bentham, 38 Political Science Quarterly, 161.

[15] Hunt, Charles H., Life of Edward Livingston, with introduction by George Bancroft; Hunt, Carleton, Life and Services of Edward Livington, Bar Association Address, reprinted 1903, 12 American Lawyer, 100, 154 (1904); *id.* Edward Livingston and the Law of Louisiana, 7 Law Notes, 88 (1903); Smith, Edward Livingston and the Louisiana Codes, 2 Columbia Law Rev. 24; Wilkinson, Edward Livingston and the Penal Codes, 1 Texas Law Rev. 25; Kent on Livingston's Penal Code, 12 American Law Rev. 480; More, The Livingston Code (1912), Journal of Criminal Law and Criminology, 344; Franklin, Concerning the Historic Importance of Edward Livington, 11 Tulane Law Rev. 163; Hall, Edward Livingston and His Louisiana Penal Code, 22 Am. Bar Assn. Journ. 191; Flory, Edward Livingston's Place in Louisiana Law, 19 Louisiana Historical Quarterly, 328. There is a full bibliography of Livingston in 11 Tulane Law Review 331 to 343.

[16] Field, H. M., Life of David Dudley Field; Obituary in 17 Rep. Am. Bar Assn., 517; Brown, David Dudley Field, 3 Green Bag, 49; Hall, Reminiscences of David Dudley Field, 6 Green Bag, 204; Fiero, David Dudley Field and His Work, 18 Rep. N. Y. State Bar Assn. 177.

[17] See Pound, Common Law and Legislation, 21 Harvard Law Rev. 383; Landis, Statutes and the Sources of Law, Harvard Legal Essays, 213.

[18] See Pound, Liberty of Contract, 18 Yale Law Journ. 454, 466–7, citing cases.

[19] Hoar, Autobiography of Seventy Years, II, 363–6.

[20] Luther Stearns Cushing, translator of Savigny on Possession (1838). See Cushing, Introduction to the Study of Roman Law, p. v. and §§ 269–74.

[21] Carter, The Ideal and the Actual in Law, 10–11; *id.*

Law: Its Origin, Growth and Function, lects. 1–8; Pomeroy, The True Method of Interpreting the Civil Code, 3 West Coast Reporter 585, 691, 717; 4 *id.* 1, 49, 109, 145, especially 147 ff.; Burdick, The Revival of Benthamite Codification, 10 Columbia Law Rev. 118, 123, 125–126. For examples of the devitalizing of statutes by treating them as declaratory of pre-existing law, see Montagu, Proposals for the Revision of the Anti-Trust Laws, in Handler, The Federal Anti-Trust Laws, a Symposium (1932), 49, n. 9. See also Tobriner and Jaffe, Revision of the Anti-Trust Laws, 20 Calif. Law Review 585, 595, n. 9.

[22] *E.g.* Bertolf *v.* O'Reilly, 74 N. Y. 509.

[23] See an excellent statement of Bentham's doctrine: Dicey, Law and Public Opinion in England, 2 ed. 134–149.

[24] *E.g.* Social Statics (1892 ed.) 197–216.

[25] *E.g.* Markby, Elements of Law, §§ 48–59.

[26] 1 Blackstone, Commentaries, 85–6.

[27] See Freund, Legislative Regulation, chap. 3; Binney, Restrictions upon Local and Special Legislation in State Constitutions; Anderson, Special Legislation in Minnesota, 7 Minnesota Law Rev. 133, 187; Reinsch, American Legislatures and Legislative Methods, 399–410. State *v.* Somers Point, 52 New Jersey Law, 32; People *v.* Gilbert, 226 N. Y. 103; Cahill *v.* Hogan, 180 N. Y. 304; Matter of Application of Paul, 94 N. Y. 497; Matter of the Application of Church, 92 N. Y. 1; Matter of the Petition of Blodgett, 89 N. Y. 392; People *v.* Newburgh, etc. Plank Road Co., 86 N. Y. 1; Huber *v.* People, 49 N. Y. 132; Gaskin *v.* Meek, 42 N. Y. 186; State *v.* Sayre, 162 Ala. 641; Town of McGregor *v.* Baylies, 19 Ia. 43; Kelley *v.* Consolidated Gas Co., 153 Md. 523, 536; State *v* County Commissioners, 19 Md. 516; State *v.* Chambers, 93 N. C. 600; Davis *v.* Clark, 106 Pa. St. 377; City of Topeka *v.* Gillette, 32 Kan. 431; Evans *v.* Phillips, 117 Pa. St. 226; Maxwell *v.* Tillamook County, 20 Or. 495; Gaither *v.* Jackson, 147 Md. 655;

Campbell's Case, 2 Bland Ch. (Md.) 209; Lee *v.* Bude & Torrington Junction R. Co., L. R. 6 C. P. 577; Holt *v.* Mayor of Birmingham, 111 Ala. 369, 373; People *v.* Central P. R. Co., 43 Cal. 398, 433; State *v.* Shearer, 46 Ohio St. 275; McGill *v.* State, 34 Ohio St. 228, 237; State *v.* Cooley, 56 Minn. 540; St. John *v.* Andrews Institute, 191 N. Y. 254, 269; State *v.* Daniel, 87 Fla. 270, 287; Dawson *v.* Payer, 5 Hare, 415.

[28] Tuskaloosa Bridge Co. *v.* Olmstead, 41 Ala. 1, 19; Langdon *v.* Applegate, 5 Ind. 327; Bay-Shell Road Co. *v.* O'Donnell, 87 Ala. 376; Bask *v.* City of Indianapolis, 120 Ind. 476; People *v.* Mahaney, 13 Mich. 481; Evernham *v.* Hulit, 45 N. J. Law, 53; State *v.* Beddo, 22 Utah, 432; Southern P. R. Co. *v.* Bartine, 170 Fed. 725; Lyons *v.* Police Pension Board, 255 Ill. 139; Timm *v.* Harrison, 109 Ill. 593, 597; Davis *v.* State, 7 Md. 151.

Leard *v.* Leard, 30 Ind. 171; Savings Bank *v.* Burns, 104 Cal. 473, 478; Minter *v.* State, 145 Tenn. 678; Queen *v.* Wilcock, 7 Q. B. 317; Murphy *v.* Webb, 156 N. C. 402; Burge *v.* Mangum, 134 Ga. 306; State *v.* Malheur County Court, 54 Or. 255; Van Dyke *v.* Thompson, 136 Tenn. 136; Batchellor *v.* Palmer, 129 Wash. 150, 154; New York C. R. Co. *v.* Stevenson, 277 Ill. 474; People *v.* Mahaney, 23 Mich. 481; Lehman *v.* McBride, 15 Ohio St. 573.

[29] State *v.* District Court, 49 Mont. 146; People *v.* State Contract Commissioners, 120 Ill. 322; Chicago, B. & Q. R. Co. *v.* Smyth, 103 Fed. 376; State *v.* Burlington & M. R. Co., 60.Neb. 741, 747–748; Parkinson *v.* State, 14 Md. 184, 193–198; Blair *v.* Chicago, 201 U. S. 400, 452; Phillips *v.* Covington Bridge Co., 2 Metc. (Ky.) 219, 221; Posendas *v.* Warner, 279 U. S. 340, 343–345; International Shoe Co. *v.* Shartel, 279 U. S. 429, 434–435; Cook *v.* Marshall County, 119 Ia. 396; Worcester County *v.* School Com'rs, 113 Md. 305; Savings Bank *v.* State, 228 Mich. 316; Burlington *v.* Pennsylvania R. Co., 104 N. J. Law, 649; Gibson *v.* State,

214 Ala. 38; Central R. Co. *v.* State, 104 Ga. 831; Moore, Mansfield Construction Co. *v.* Indianapolis etc. R. Co., 179 Ind. 356; State *v.* Burgdoefer, 107 Mo. 1; Stockton *v.* Central R. Co., 50 N. J. Eq. 52; Neuersdorff *v.* Duryea, 69 N. Y. 557; Com. *v.* Brown, 91 Va. 762; Com. *v.* Robinson, 192 Ky. 374; Weber *v.* Probey, 125 Md. 544; Investors' Realty Co. *v.* Harrisburg, 281 Pa. St. 200; Wilson *v.* State, 143 Tenn. 55; Wallace *v.* Zinman, 200 Cal. 585; Williams *v.* Atchison etc. R. Co., 233 Mo. 666; Weil *v.* State, 46 Ohio St. 450; Long *v.* Harrison County, 114 Miss. 341.

[30] *E.g.* Hovey *v.* State, 119 Ind. 395.

[31] *E.g.* State *v.* Cannon, 206 Wis. 374.

[32] *Ex parte* Griffiths, 118 Ind. 83. Cf. Houston *v.* Williams, 13 Cal. 24.

[33] See Pound, Coöperation in Enforcement of Law, Proceedings of Third Annual Meeting of the State Bar of California, 63–77, 16 Am. Bar Assn. Journal, 9.

[34] Hosmer, C. J. in Goshen *v.* Stonington, 4 Conn. 209, 225.

[35] Jackson, J. in Holden *v.* James, 11 Mass. 396, 405.

[36] State Bank *v.* Cooper, 2 Yerger (Tenn.) 599.

[37] 8 Rep. 114, 118.

[38] Hob. 85, 87.

[39] 12 Mod. 669, 687.

[40] Miller, J. in Loan Assn. *v.* Topeka, 20 Wall. (U. S.) 655, 663. Mr. Justice Miller's statement is at least reminiscent of § 2 of the Bill of Rights in the Kentucky Constitution of 1850: "Arbitrary power does not exist anywhere in a free government."

[41] See Beutel, The Necessity of a New Technique of Interpreting the Negotiable Instruments Law, 6 Tulane Law Rev. 1.

[42] Pound, Common Law and Legislation, 21 Harvard Law Rev. 383; Allen, Law in the Making, 256–259. Compare the rule as to interpretation of penal statutes: Hall, Strict or

Liberal Construction of Penal Statutes, 48 Harvard Law Rev. 748.

[43] Holland, Jurisprudence, 12 ed. 76, n. 2. For a typical example of ignorant legislation of the sort which has had much to do with the attitude of the legal profession, see Dolphin *v.* Worcester Consol. St. Ry. Co., 189 Mass. 270. Here the statute, in an attempt to change the existing rule, through ignorance of the draftsman used such language as to require a less degree of care on the part of carriers of passengers than that required by the common law. One need not say that the statute was repealed at the next session of the legislature.

[44] Collected Essays, 211.

[45] Federal Interpleader Act of 1917, 39 Stat. 929, now superseded by the Act of 1926, 44 Stat. 416.

[46] See Chafee, Interpleader in the United States Courts, 41 Yale Law Journ. 1134, 42 *id.* 41; Chafee, Federal Interpleader Bill: Draft and Memorandum, 59 Rep. Am. Bar Assn. 68.

[47] Lindsay *v.* Candy, 10 Q. B. D. 348; Queen *v.* Commissioners under the Boiler Explosions Act [1891], 1 Q. B. 703; State *v.* Standard Oil Co., 61 Ore. 438; Com. *v.* Fulton, 263 Pa. St. 332; Robinson *v.* Local Board of Barton Eccles, 21 Ch. D. 621, 8 App. Cas. 798; Queen *v.* Pearce, 5 Q. B. D. 388.

[48] Application of Monrovia Evening Post, 199 Cal. 263; Midland R. Co. *v.* Ambergate R. Co., 10 Hare, 359.

[49] See State *v.* Ruesswig, 110 Minn. 473; State *v.* Partlow, 91 N. C. 550; People *v.* Patten, 338 Ill. 385; State *v.* West Side St. R. Co., 146 Mo. 155; Hallman *v.* Coker, 147 Ark. 73; People *v.* Sweitzer, 266 Ill. 459.

[50] People *v.* Patten, *supra;* Hallman *v.* Coker, *supra.*

[51] People *v.* Sweitzer, *supra.*

[52] State *v.* Partlow, *supra.*

[53] State *v.* West Side St. R. Co., *supra.*

[54] Hallman *v.* Coker, *supra.*

[55] Pound, Juristic Problems of National Progress, 22 American Journal of Sociology, 721; Pound, Anachronisms in Law, 3 Journal of the American Judicature Society, 142, 146; Pound, Criminal Justice in the American City, Criminal Justice in Cleveland, 605–606; Pound, Criminal Justice in America, 208, 209. See Bentham, Works (Bowring ed.), IX, 597–612; Ferri, Criminal Sociology, transl. by Morrison, 153; Nash, Life of Lord Westbury, I, 191; Report of Lord Haldane's Committee on the Machinery of Government (1918); Cardozo, A Ministry of Justice, 35 Harvard Law Rev. 113; Glueck, The Ministry of Justice and the Problem of Crime, 4 American Review, 139; Reports of the Commission to Investigate Defects in the Law and Its Administration, New York Legislative Documents, nos. 70 (1924), 74 (1925); Mullins, The Quest of Justice, 420–428; Yntema, Legal Science and Reform, 34 Columbia Law Rev. 207, 215–230; The Ministry of Justice and the Statute Law Commission, 5 Law Magazine and Review (2d series) 352; Bacon, A Ministry of Justice, 22 Virginia Law Rev. 175.

[56] Pound, Common Law and Legislation, 21 Harvard Law Rev. 383. See also Stone, The Common Law in the United States, in The Future of the Common Law, 120, 130–135.

III

JUDICIAL DECISION

IT will have been noted that in these lectures the emphasis is put on historical continuity of the taught legal tradition. This tradition, received from England, to no small extent through a few leaders in each of the colonies who had been trained in the Inns of Court,[1] and transmitted by generations of lawyers trained under the apprentice system, likewise received from England, was taught later in law schools which preserved much of that system and continued to hand down that tradition. It was not till the present century that the academic type of law school definitely prevailed and the apprentice type ceased to train the bulk of those who came to the bar from law schools. It was not till the present generation that law-school training definitely superseded apprentice training in the offices of practitioners as preparation for the bar. The dogmatic teaching which prevailed in law office and in the apprentice type of law school made for an obstinate legal tradition.

One might tell the story of the formulating agencies of the law in our formative era with the emphasis on change rather than continuity. If we look only at the body of legal precepts which obtains in the United States today in comparison with those obtaining in seventeenth or even eighteenth century England, we might easily feel that the change has been radical and complete. But change has been gradual, has been chiefly in details, and hence not to be understood without understanding what was changed, and has been guided by the received traditional technique, applied to received traditional materials. Thus much that has been changed has continued to furnish analogies and to serve as the basis of legal reasoning and even to affect the newer precepts in their interpretation and application.

Tenacity of a taught legal tradition is much more significant in our legal history than the economic conditions of time and place. These conditions have by no means been uniform, while the course of decision has been characteristically steady and uniform, hewing to common-law lines through five generations of rapid political, economic and social change, and bringing about a *communis opinio* over the country as a whole on the overwhelming majority of legal questions, despite the most divergent geographical, political, economic, social and even racial conditions. Today national law schools, teaching law, not laws, and teaching law in the "spirit of the common legal heritage of English-speaking peoples," are working effectively to preserve this uniformity, against many forces of disintegration.

Economic and political conditions of time and place have led to legislative abrogations and alternations of rules and even at times to attempts to alter the course of the taught tradition. But such changes are fitted into the traditional system in their interpretation and application, and affect slowly or very little the principles, conceptions and doctrines which are the enduring law. The outstanding phenomenon is the extent to which a taught tradition, in the hands of judges drawn from any class one will, and chosen as one will, so they have been trained in the tradition, has stood out against all manner of economically or politically powerful interests. The role of economics in our legal history has not been one of dictating decision of particular causes or judicial promulgation of particular new rules, but one of raising new wants, new claims, new demands and desires. The pressure of new interests has required that the taught tradition be made to serve new purposes as old doctrines were called on to solve new problems. There has been a gradual shaping of obstinate traditional precepts and traditional doctrines through the need of applying them to new economic conditions in the light of reshaping ideals of the legal order. Old analogies are developed by the traditional technique to meet problems arising from newly pressing unrecognized and unsecured interests. The law is slow in responding to such pressure, no matter what class is affected. The American man of business, the captain of industry, has had as much cause of complaint in this respect as the laborer; [2] and the farmer, long dominant politically in our pioneer communities, as much cause as either.[3] Reason is applied to experience to work out adjustments of relations under new conditions. Also reason, applied abstractly to new conditions, is corrected by experience. Moreover, this is done by applying a received technique to received precepts and doctrines.

Thus the common law proves to have a vitality demonstrated in a long succession of contests with the most powerful political and economic forces of time and place.[4]

Take three great judges of the formative era of our law, Lemuel Shaw, John Bannister Gibson and Thomas Ruffin. Shaw [5] was a staunch Federalist; son of a Congregational minister in a poor parish — so poor that part of the minister's salary was paid in fire wood and the money payments were always in arrear and the accumulated arrears were never paid. He was brought up in a community of farmers and fishermen on Cape Cod, was a graduate of Harvard, a school teacher and newspaper writer, while reading for the bar, and lived in his maturity in the stable commercial environment of Boston of that day.

Gibson [6] was a Democrat of Jackson's type (Jackson wished to put him on the Supreme Court of the United States), the son of a prosperous and successful man of business in a frontier community, who was also a colonel in the Revolutionary army. He was brought up after his father's death by his mother who (since her husband's fortunes had been altered in the depression after the Revolution) had a hard struggle to maintain the family mansion and the mill her husband had operated, and to set up and conduct a school in order that her children might be educated. He studied at Dickinson College but did not graduate. He practised law in a developing community and associated while at the bar with the enterprizing builders of a relatively new region. He evaded baptism by going hunting at the time his mother had set, and was not active in any church.

Ruffin [7] was a conservative Democrat, born and reared on a plantation in Virginia. He graduated at Princeton. He was by descent and bringing up one of the landed aristocracy of the old South and in his maturity lived upon his own plantation among his fellow gentlemen planters. He was a zealous member of the Episcopal Church.

Each of these men long dominated the highest court of an important state, from which many newer states took their legal traditions and upon whose decisions these newer states built their course of decision. The differences in their parentage, bringing up, social environment, political affiliations, and economic surroundings should, according to the psychological and economic determinists of today, have determined their judicial action decisively and so have led to three different judicial traditions. Yet they co-operated in making a consistent body of law on the basis of the tradition they had been taught in the offices of lawyers whose training (through office apprenticeship) ran back to barristers trained in the Inns of Court.

Pressure of new demands, problems created by the development of transportation, the effect of inventions, and the rise of industry in some sections and growth of trade in others, called for new reasoned applications of the technique in which these judges had been trained to the body of legal precepts and established legal analogies which had been taught them. This, rather than the Marxian class struggle is the economic interpretation of

American law in its formative era. One of the stock arguments of the American economic determinists is drawn from Shaw's opinion in Farwell *v.* Boston & Worcester R. R. Corp.,[8] in which the fellow servant rule, established by a well known English decision, was received for America. This is spoken of as if it set up an arbitrary exception to a rule of law which expressed a fundamental and universal idea of justice. It did nothing of the sort. It refused to extend further an exception to a then generally received doctrine that liability must flow from fault.[9] It would have been quite impossible for American judges trained in the common-law tradition, acting in the light of the received ideals of the times, to come to any other conclusion. Moreover, in Commonwealth *v.* Hunt,[10] the same Chief Justice Shaw, in the same year, decided a leading case on the law of conspiracy in favor of the labor unions and "overthrew the substructure upon which a Tory criminal law against labor organizations could respectably have been established." [11] The proponents of economic determinism, looking at these two decisions by the same court in the same year, can only say that fear of a radical movement in politics dictated the second decision.[12] But the testimony of those who knew Shaw is unanimous and decisive that "it was impossible to imagine him swayed by prejudice or popular clamor." [13] Moreover, Shaw's associates, who concurred in the "liberal" decision in Commonwealth *v.* Hunt, were Samuel S. Wilde, an old line Federalist, who had been a member of the Hartford Convention,[14] Charles Dewey, who had been brought up in the office of that obstinate Federalist and aristocrat Theodore Sedgwick,[15] and Samuel Hubbard, an appointee of the "Federalist-Whigs."[16] One can imagine how this would have been played up by the economic determinists had the decision gone the other way. It seems to be impossible for a Marxian economic determinist to comprehend an honest man. When one studies the history of the law as to conspiracy and the relation of Hawkins's doctrine (relied upon by those who prosecuted labor unions as conspiracies) to received professional ideals of the social order in America, it is perfectly possible to understand Farwell *v.* Boston & Worcester R. R. Corp. and Commonwealth *v.* Hunt without attributing political motives to a man whose whole judicial career is a refutation of such a charge.

On another occasion I have spoken more fully of the attempt of a leader among American teachers of law to give an economic interpretation of a well known English case requiring those who maintain upon their land things liable to escape and do damage to restrain such things at their peril of answering for resulting damage if they escape.[17] The thesis is that the land owning gentry were the dominant class in England in 1868 and that the idea of land as a permanent family acquisition, not as something to be used for profit, underlies the decision. One might remark that the judge whose view seems to have had the most weight was by no means sprung from a county family, and that his practice had been in commercial causes.[18] The economic feature would have had no great appeal for him, and, in fact, he merely applied by analogy a well settled line of reasoning in the old cases. But the argument is that in America the business man represented the dominant class and so his idea of land as something, like all other property, to be used for profit dictated American rejection of the English rule.[19] However, all American courts did not reject it. It has been followed in Massachusetts, Minnesota, Ohio, West Virginia, Missouri, and Texas,[20] and rejected in New Hampshire, New York, New Jersey, Pennsylvania, California, Kentucky, and Indiana.[21] No possible economic reasons can explain this division of opinion. But the student of American legal doctrine will note at once that Massachusetts habitually followed English authority and was followed as a matter of course in some states, while a masterful judge in New Hampshire reexamined the question in the light of a general principle of no tort liability without fault and his decision convinced the New York Court of Appeals, which is habitually followed in many other jurisdictions.

A good example of a difference of judicial opinion in different states, may be seen in the decisions as to the risk of loss in an executory contract for the sale of land. An English decision, going on the doctrine of what is called conversion and equitable ownership, put the risk upon the purchaser.[22] This was followed by the Supreme Court of the United States [23] and in ten states,[24] partly on the basis of authority, but chiefly because it followed from the conception of the consequences of a vendor purchaser relation as held by courts of equity. In Massachusetts, however, there was for a long time no equity jurisdiction and complete equity powers did not exist in the courts till 1877. Accordingly the Supreme Court of Massachusetts could not appreciate the reasoning of the English case and held in 1838 that the risk was on the vendor.[25] Seven courts, some of them accustomed to follow Massachusetts, others troubled by a rule which, even if demanded by analytical reasoning, seemed to run counter to the everyday understanding of men, adopted the view of loss falling on the vendor.[26] An economic interpretation distinguishing California from Oregon, Georgia from Alabama, Kansas from Iowa, is out of the question. But from the standpoint of doctrinal history the basis of the two lines of authority and of a suggested compromise is quite understandable.[27]

Undoubtedly American legislation of the formative era may be understood to a large extent through a conventional economic interpretation. But only to a large extent for two reasons. One is that much of that legislation was declaratory of what had in principle, if not in rule, become part of the judicial tradition. A second is that legislation enacted arbitrarily at the instance of some group or class was always tempered or restrained in its operation in the course of judicial interpretation and application. Nor were the judges inclined to follow legislative legal anomalies by analogy. Popularly elected legislators might yield to pressure from a politically dominant class of farmers and make promissory notes payable in corn and potatoes negotiable.[28] No popularly elected bench ever followed that example.

As an agency of growth in the shaping of American law, judicial decision did not have the advantage of public confidence at the outset and a long start as legislation did. Where the English courts had stood for the rights of Englishmen against the crown, it had been the colonial legislatures which stood for the rights of the colonists against crown and royal governors. There was much distrust of judges. The time of colonization, the seventeenth century, saw the nadir of the bench in England under Charles II and James II, and a bad tradition of judges was brought to the New World.[29] Ideas bred by experience of Whigs and dissenters in England were reinforced by experience of colonists with royal judges in America. Hence judicial organization went forward slowly and the personnel of the bench for some time was not such as to make judicial decision an active creative agency. In Massachusetts, of ten chief justices and twenty-three associates between 1692 and 1776, only one chief justice and two associate justices were lawyers.[30] Two of the three justices of the highest court of New Jersey during the Revolution were not lawyers.[31] Of the three justices in New Hampshire after independence, one was a clergyman and another a physician.[32] A blacksmith sat on the highest court of Rhode Island from 1814 to 1818, and a farmer was chief justice of that state from 1819 to 1826.[33] There are no reports of American judicial decision of any consequence till the last decade of the eighteenth century, and regular reporting begins in the nineteenth century.[34]

But the legal materials available to courts and lawyers were English. The French and Dutch books on natural law gave them guiding ideas. But Blackstone and Coke gave usable legal precepts for everyday use. As lawyers cited and law students studied them, a taught tradition became established, and such a tradition makes enduring law. Thus the common-law technique of finding the grounds of decision in reported judicial experience became the decisive agency of law making in our formative era. Even in Louisiana, where the civil-law background might have put doctrinal writing where it then was in Continental Europe, judicial decision became controlling.

There are many signs that American law has entered on a period of creative activity analogous to the two classical creative eras in our legal history — the seventeenth century which made the feudal land law of medieval England into a system which could go round the world in the nineteenth century, and the time after the Revolution when English legal institutions and doctrines and precepts were made over to conform to an ideal of American society by a criterion of applicability to American conditions. In each of these creative eras lawyers had a lively faith that they could do things by conscious effort intelligently directed. In each they were guided by a philosophical theory of natural law. In each they turned to some extent to comparative law to give concrete content to abstract ideas of natural law. In each they sought to bring the legal and the moral into accord, and thus brought into the authoritative legal materials much from outside of the law.

On every hand there are signs of a revival of this faith in the efficacy of effort, in marked contrast with the juristic pessimism of a generation ago. Interest in philosophy of law is notably reviving in all English-speaking lands. Comparative law is taking on new life. Jurists everywhere are seeking a canon of values which is in some degree restoring the old consciousness of the relation of law to morals.

History of a system of law is largely a history of borrowings of legal materials from other legal systems and of assimilation of materials from outside of the law. In the history of Anglo-American law there are successive borrowings and adaptations from Roman law (*e.g.* the rules as to title by occupation), from the canon law (*e.g.* our law and practice as to marriage and divorce and probate and administration), from the modern Roman law and Continental codes (*e.g.* in our law of riparian rights), and from the commercial law of Continental Europe, as Mansfield's decisions and the decisions and texts of Kent and Story make clear abundantly. Also there are successive assimilations and adaptations from outside of the law: from the Frankish administrative regime, as in the origin of the jury; from the sixteenth and seventeenth-century Continental administrative regime, as in the common law of misdemeanors through the Star Chamber; from scholasticism in the fourteenth and fifteenth centuries, as in the Aristotelian theory of common-law maxims in Fortescue and Littleton; from sixteenth-century casuist literature in equity, as shown in Doctor and Student; from the law-of-nature philosophy in the seventeenth century, as in the doctrine of reformation in equity where there has been defective execution of an attempt to perform a moral duty; from the general usage of the mercantile world, as in the law of negotiable instruments; and from the current custom of the time and place, as in the British law as to crossing of checks or our American mining law. In all these cases it is the form and shape that has been made by the lawmaking agencies, not the content. The content was found. The form was given authoritatively. For except as an act of omnipotence, creation is not the making of something out of nothing. In legal history it is the reshaping of traditional legal materials, the bringing in of other materials from without and the adaptation of these materials as a whole to the securing of human claims and satisfaction of human wants under new conditions of life in civilized society. The creative process consists in going outside of the authoritative legal materials of the time and place, or even outside of the law, and selecting something which is then combined with or added to the existing materials, or the existing methods of developing and applying those materials, and is then gradually given form as a legal precept or legal doctrine or legal institution. In Jhering's apt phrase, the process is one of juristic chemistry.[35] The chemist does not make the materials which go into his test tube. He selects them and combines them for some purpose and his purpose thus gives form to the result.

In the formative era of our law such a process went on under the criterion of applicability to American conditions by which our courts judged English rules and doctrines and institutions in order to determine whether they were received by us as common law and, in case they were not applicable, to determine what should obtain in their place. How was the applicability of English legal precepts to American conditions to be determined? There were no rules defining it. That English legal precepts were in force with us so far as they were applicable, and only so far as applicable, was not a principle with any such historically-given definiteness of content as the principle that harm intentionally caused is actionable unless justified, by means of which courts and jurists have been writing a new chapter in our law of torts in the last generation. Nor was there any traditional technique of receiving the law of one country as the law of another which our courts could lay hold of and utilize. What they did was to determine what was applicable and what was not applicable to America by reference to an idealized picture of pioneer, rural, agricultural America of the fore part of the nineteenth century, and this picture became part of the law.[86]

Again, when our courts were called upon to perform the novel task of interpreting written constitutions and judging of legislative acts with reference to constitutional texts, something they could not but feel was different in kind from the interpretation of statutes, they had no traditional technique at hand. As in all interpretations, the "spirit" of constitutional texts or the "spirit" of constitutions began to be invoked and it became necessary to give a content to abstract constitutional formulas exactly as the civilian has had to give a content for modern purposes to abstract oracular texts of the Roman books. Our traditional art of deciding had not had to do with such problems. Except for Coke's exposition of Magna Carta and of the legislation of Edward I, there had been little to do in the way of building a system of legal precepts upon a foundation of authoritative texts. Moreover Coke's Second Institute was in great part a political tract in the contest of the common-law courts with the Stuarts. The influence of Coke's exposition upon judicial application of our bills of rights is obvious. The most significant legal provisions of the bills of rights were taken from the Second Institute and represent an attempt to give to the natural rights of men a concrete content of the immemorial common-law rights of Englishmen, as set forth by Coke and Blackstone. Yet this historico-philosophical content, derived from seventeenth-century England and eighteenth-century France, could not be used, as it came to us, as a measure of American legislative power. Hence the courts worked out an idea of "the nature of free government" or "the nature of American government" or "the nature of American institutions" — an idealized picture of the legal and political institutions of pioneer America.[37]

Likewise, when in the last quarter of the nineteenth century our courts were called upon with increasing frequency to pass on the validity of social legislation, in the transition from pioneer, rural, agricultural America to the urban, industrial America of today, they made use of an idealized picture of the economic order with which they were familiar, the principles of which had been set forth by the classical political economists. They pictured an ideal society in which there was a maximum of abstract free individual self-assertion. This they postulated as "liberty" as secured in bills of rights.

Hence all limitations upon abstract free self-assertion, all derogation from a maximum of such self-assertion was presumably arbitrary. They held that such legislation sought vainly to turn back the current of legal progress in its steady flow from status to contract and so was not due process of law.

Early in the last century Chief Justice Marshall reminded us that the founders of our legal polity "were intimately acquainted with the writings of those wise and learned men whose treatises on the law of nature and nations have guided public opinion in the subjects of obligation and contracts." [38] He argued that the idea of natural law, and hence of the legally binding force of the moral obligation of contract, maintained in these treatises, must be the basis of applying the contract clause in the Federal Constitution. As I said in the first lecture, the law-of-nature theory prevailed universally among lawyers well into the nineteenth century. Law in the sense of the analytical theory, the body of legal precepts bearing the guinea stamp of the state, was taken to be but an imperfect reflection of an ultimate and universal natural law. It was an attempt to realize an ideal of what law should be, founded on rational consideration of human nature, and a resulting picture of an ideal human society. One of the chief characteristics of this natural-law jurisprudence was its identification of law and morals.

What, as the particular jurist saw it, ought to be law, because it ought to be law was law.

Reaction from the seventeenth and eighteenth-century identification of law and morals is a marked feature of every type of nineteenth-century juristic thought. Philosophical jurists contrasted them. Analytical jurists insisted on keeping them apart. To them only legal precepts which had actually received the stamp of the state's authority and were enforced in tribunals were law. Everything else was matter for a separate science of legislation or for ethics. They pointed with something like pride to cases which seemed to show that one could have a legal right which was morally wrong. They were never weary of refuting the proposition that a legal right is not a right if it is not right. This mode of thinking bore fruit in the mechanical jurisprudence which was at its height in this country about 1875.[39]

All this in its day was a sound corrective of the loose notions as to the basis of legal obligation in the inherent moral force of the just legal precept, of the individual conscience as the measure of all moral and hence of all legal obligation, and of the possibility of devising a perfect code by reasoning from purely moral premises, with which the eighteenth-century treatises are filled. But after the manner of reactions it went too far. For the analytical conception of legal duty is not a conception found in the law by analysis. It is a conception taken over into the law from ethics and but partially legalized. Historically it goes back to the Stoic conception of the course of conduct which accords with nature, that is, with ideal perfection — the conduct of a perfect man because he is perfect. Roman lawyers in effect made this a legal conception but they never discuss it as such. In form it remains a purely moral conception. The Roman lawyers simply gave it a legal content.[40] This bit of history is repeated in English law, as one may see readily in the pages of Doctor and Student and in the old equity cases.[41] We must recognize today that the rigid setting off of what was called law from the ideal of law has proved a disservice in blinding us for two generations to factors of the first moment in the actual working of the legal order. It has led to a merely superficial certainty. It has brought about a belief in a mechanical logical application of fixed legal precepts which expresses only a part of the truth. It has produced in the present a condition of groping for method where, if we had recognized what we were doing, we might have utilized the experience of our formative era and might in a new creative era have been proceeding more intelligently.

On the breakdown of the natural-law philosophy at the end of the eighteenth century, the ideal philosophical pattern was replaced in general use by an ideal analytical pattern or a historical pattern or a combination of the two. The analytical pattern postulated a body of logically interdependent legal precepts commanded or authoritatively recognized by the state or derivable by a logical process from precepts so commanded or so recognized. The historical pattern was one of a body of traditional principles and conceptions representing the unfolding of an idea of right or an idea of freedom in human experience of the administration of justice and fixing for all time the lines of legal development. But a philosophical pattern persisted to a certain extent. Putting them in the order in which chronologically they affect American judicial decision in the last century, we may recognize five theories. They are: (1) The law-of-nature theory in different stages of decay; (2) the analytical or imperative theory; (3) the historical or traditional theory; (4) the metaphysical theory or theory of deductions from rights as corollaries of liberty, and (5) a positivist theory in various forms.

We began to import the natural-law theory and to put it to work as an instrument both of shaping our received legal materials and of furnishing grounds of decision at a time when it was already moribund.[42] The most pressing problem of our formative era was to work out and lay down rules;

to provide an apparatus of legal precepts equal to the requirements of expanding American life. This problem determined our system of courts, our judicial organization, and in large part the course of our legal development until the last quarter of the nineteenth century. It was less important to decide particular causes justly than to work out sound, logically consistent and abstractly just rules for the future. For about a century the chief energies of our courts were directed to the development of a body of law in each of our jurisdictions by means of judicial decision. The function of ascertaining and declaring the law became the most important part of judicial activity. An elaborate succession of appeals and new trials sought to insure that the grounds of the ultimate decision should be so elaborately worked out and carefully formulated as to give a clear precedent. The theory of natural law was peculiarly adapted to this purpose, and, as new commonwealths were set up in successive waves of our westward expansion, the theory was given new life or new form until, only yesterday, the work of judicial development of a common law for our newest commonwealths had been substantially achieved. Thus the natural-law theory was kept alive in America long after it had ceased to be a living theory in the Old World because we had to use judicial decision as a means of furnishing a body of law for a succession of new jurisdictions.

I have spoken of the stabilizing influence of natural law. One of the stabilizing factors in the formative era in America was identification of the natural rights of man, as declared by the Continental jurists, with the immemorial common-law rights of Englishmen as declared by Coke and Blackstone.[43] In the natural-law identification of law with morals, the moral duties of a perfect man in an abstract state of perfection, and the qualities of such a man in such a state, whereby he ought to have certain things and do certain things, furnished an absolute and universal system of legal duties and legal rights. The great juristic achievement of the nineteenth century is the thorough working out of a system of individual legal rights, and that achievement has its roots deep in this theory. But the American common-law jurisdictions, with no apparatus of centuries of interpretation of the Roman texts to fall back upon, and with no assurance how far English legal materials had been received and were in force, had to give a certain fundamental concrete content to natural rights at the outset and at once. We did this by taking our philosophical mold from Grotius and Pufendorf and Vattel and Burlamaqui and pouring into that mold a concrete content from Coke's Second Institute and Blackstone's Commentaries. We set up an ideal development of the immemorial common-law rights of Englishmen, as defined by Coke and by Blackstone following him, as a universal natural law. Thus we gave form and direction to our judicial working out of a system of legal rights adapted to the new world. But in contrast to the classical natural law it was a political and legal, not an ethical form and direction. Natural law was made a force for fixity in legal development, not a liberalizing force as it was with Mansfield, with the Continental jurists of the seventeenth century, and even with Pothier.

Three other phases of the natural-law theory in the formative era of American law likewise made for stability in the law shaped by judicial decision. In the first place we began almost at the outset to identify natural law with an ideal form of the positive law. In theory the positive law was valid only in so far as it was in accord with the universal ideal law. But in practice we judged the English law by an ideal form of itself. This was no new phenomenon. Roman jurists had given a legal content to the Greek conception of the just-by-nature in much the same way, taking an ideal rational development of the precepts of the strict law for a rational pattern of all law. Also in the seventeenth century jurists assumed that for the most part the law taught by the universities on the basis of the

Corpus Juris, with which they were familiar, was embodied reason, and hence that for the great majority of cases an ideal development of Roman principles was synonymous with the law of nature. Thus we used the theory to prune away archaisms and arbitrary rules of the strict law and to give the law logical internal consistency, exactly as the Romans had used it in the second century and as Western Europe had used it in the seventeenth century. With us, however, it was used as a mode of developing law through judicial decision, whereas at Rome and in seventeenth-century Europe it had affected the law through juristic speculation and academic teaching.

Another stabilizing influence was the idea that a universal commercial law, as set forth in the Continental treatises on that subject, was declaratory of natural law. English courts began by an actual ascertainment for each case, as a matter of fact, of what the custom of merchants actually was. Presently they began to consider what the custom of merchants ought to be. It was characteristic of the time to assume that when they had determined as a matter of reason what it ought to be, that of itself settled what it was. The Continental treatises on commercial law, on which Kent and his brethren rely on every page of Johnson's Reports, are a medley of general commercial usage, modernized Roman law, and juristic consideration of what ought to be. They served to liberalize commercial law from end to end. But they served also to stabilize the law and, in Bentham's language, to make it "cognoscible," since they gave something to which lawyers might turn with reasonable assurance both as the basis of advice and as the basis of argument.

In the third place, a conception of an ideal of comparative law as declaratory of natural law gave direction to judicial development of the law. We must not forget that reception of English law as the law of post-Revolutionary America was not a foregone conclusion, nor did it take place without a struggle. Many Americans would have liked to put the administration of justice wholly on a non-technical basis of natural equity. Many more called for rejection of the legal systems of the old world and the making of a new code of American law on the basis of the law of nature. Many would have received French law as for good reason you did in Louisiana. Not the least of the means by which Kent and Story did so much to insure the general reception of English common law was a skilful use of comparative law, seeming to show the identity of an ideal form of the common-law rule with an ideal form of the civil-law rule, and thus demonstrating the identity of each with a universally acknowledged law of nature.[44]

More of the creative spirit of seventeenth-century natural law is to be found in the doctrine that the common law was received only so far as applicable to the physical, political, social, and economic conditions of America,[45] and in a later and specialized form in which legal precepts were judged by their conformity to "the nature of American government"[46] or the "nature of American institutions."[47] In truth, what is original in the judicial working out of American common law in the formative era comes in through these ideas. Through them courts rejected inconvenient items in what they found in the English books or in the treatises on commercial law or in comparative law. Where the other identifications of natural law were instruments of borrowing and adaptation from other legal systems, these theories were agencies of developing our indigenous political and social institutions into legal materials. But before the century was out the doctrine of applicability had done its work, and the ideas of conformity to the nature of American government and conformity to the nature of American institutions had become means of holding down social legislation by subjecting it to the test of what was suited to the rural, pioneer society of the time when our institutions were formative.[48]

Taken over after it had lost its vigor elsewhere,

the theory of natural law soon entered upon a stage of decadence. It was a theory for teachers and doctrinal writers turned in America to the use of judges. Hence inevitably it tended to become stabilized. In most of the forms which it took with us from the beginning, it was creative only to the extent that it facilitated borrowing and adaptation from definite known bodies of legal precepts. Thus we may understand how easily in the last decade of the nineteenth century it could become an obstacle to growth and a check on all conscious improvement of the law.

As a theory of judicial decision, natural law, the doctrine that a court proceeded, not on a given authoritative body of legal precepts as such, but on an ideal universal body of rational principles, of which actual legal precepts were at most but declaratory, was at its best when courts were called on to utilize the peculiar social and political institutions of pioneer America in developing or supplementing the legal materials afforded by the English common law, the Continental treatises on commercial law, and comparative law. For the rest, it furnished a convenient dogmatic justification for the criterion of applicability to American conditions, for the filling up of gaps where English legal precepts were found inapplicable, and for drawing upon the Continental commercial law and upon comparative law where English legal materials were not at hand. When the process of receiving English law was complete, when there was no longer need of borrowing from European commercial law, and a prop of comparative law was not needed to reinforce English rules and institutions against political prejudice, the theory of natural law had done its work. Then it served for a season to justify the received legal precepts as they were and to set up an ideal of the common law as the legal order of nature.

In the latter part of the nineteenth century, theories of judicial decision had come to be analytical or historical or both. Jurists thought of law as the imperative of the state, applied mechanically by tribunals in the administration of justice,[49] or as a body of traditional legal precepts by which the state permitted causes to be adjudicated for the time being in the absence of its imperatives,[50] or as a body of formulations of experience of human conduct, and of experience of human administration of justice, the universal governing principles of which were to be discovered by historical inquiry.[51] It was considered that courts found the grounds of decision in the rules authoritatively prescribed, or in the traditional legal precepts embodied in judicial decisions of the past, or through logical development of the historically discovered universals. In either case the judicial function was taken to be one of discovery of the definitely appointed precept, or development of such a precept, already existing potentially in the historically discoverable universals, by an absolute method admitting of no scope for anything but logical identification of the actual or deduction of the potential legal precept and mechanical application thereof.[52] When men began to think in this fashion in the second half of the last century, the formative era was over.

In the nineteenth century the analytical jurist assumed a rigidly defined dogma of separation of powers. He assumed that judicial creative activity in modern states was at best a survival from a relatively primitive stage of legal development before a separation of powers had been achieved. He assumed that until a complete system of legislative express commands had been set up, the deficiency would be eked out by a primitive device of judge-made rules which the state impliedly imposed *ad interim* till it got around to issue express commands. He assumed that there was a difficulty in applying the analytical theory to lawmaking through judicial decision in common-law countries only because those countries keep many characteristics of an older condition in the history of law in which judicial and legislative functions were confused or undifferentiated. He assumed that if the spheres of law and of morals come into contact in judicial decision, it is because, while in a theoretically fully developed legal system judicial and legislative functions are fully separated, in practice this separation has not been completely realized.[53]

It will not have escaped your notice that when he argues thus the analytical jurist concedes that he is not going on a basis of pure fact. He is not discarding all ideals nor proceeding exclusively on "what is." He presupposes a complete analytical separation of powers and the possibility of a complete body of legal rules sufficient for every case. As to the former, the courts long ago saw that while the functions of the three departments of government are distinct at the core, there is a common area of powers of doubtful classification which, whether looked at analytically or historically or in both ways, may be referred with equal propriety to more than one department, so that it is a legitimate legislative function to assign the exercise of the power to any appropriate department.[54] As to the latter, all legal experience has demonstrated its futility. Until the world stands still and life ceases to involve activity and change, every code and every corpus juris will be subject to alteration and interpretation and revision. Nor will society remain quiescent long enough to enable a complete body of rules to be set up even for one time and place.

Historical theories of judicial decision begin to affect American law after the Civil War and are dominant in the last decades of the nineteenth century and in the first decade of the present century. In law, as in everything else, the nineteenth century is the century of history. The historical theory of law is the characteristic nineteenth-century theory. It came later with us because there was creative work to be done in American law after the creative energy that followed Renaissance and Reformation was spent in other lands. Historical jurisprudence was a passive restraining mode of thought on legal subjects by way of reaction from the active creative thought of the era of philosophy. It was a reaction, too, from the confident disregard of traditional legal institutions and conditions of time and place which characterized the French Revolution. We were not ready for it in the fore part of the last century. But we accepted it eagerly toward the end of that century when it was already moribund in Europe.

According to the historical theory, a decision, so far as it declared the law, was the culmination for the time being of a process of development in which an idea was unfolding or realizing itself. Hence the result in practice was to tie down judicial empiricism, and to restrain judicial discovery of the workable rule through trial and error. It projected an analysis of the law of one time back into history and then made it a rigid measure of legal history for all time. Moreover the idea, conceived as unfolding in legal history, got its philosophical content from the nineteenth-century metaphysical jurists and its legal content from ideals of the society of the time and place. Thus in the individualist society of the last century the individual free will was made the central point in the theory of law.[55]

This conception of the end of law in terms of metaphysics and individualist economics first influenced English text writers on the law of contracts, who persistently sought to mold the law to Savigny's theory of giving effect to the declared will, thereby realizing the freedom of the declarant by making his will operative in the external world. Often they succeeded in inducing the courts to follow them, and American writers presently took up the theory, partly from the English texts and partly from English decisions.[56] In the same way text writers and courts following them attempted to restate the common law of public callings in terms of the modern Roman-law theory of a legal giving effect to the will of contracting parties.[57] Even more they went a long way toward making over the Anglo-American law of torts by a modern Roman-law generalization of no liability without fault.[58] That generalization could not be made to explain all the phenomena of liability for tort at common law. But such things as were not consistent with it were pronounced "historical anomalies" and jurists were declaring that liability without fault was moribund at the very time when it was showing a remarkable vitality in the reports.[59] The net result in judicial decision was to keep the law of contracts for a time out of line with the ideas of a business world, to hold back the development of a law of public utilities, and to confuse a development of the law of torts in accord with the demands of life in a crowded world.

A second characteristic of the historical theory is what I have called juristic pessimism; a conviction of the futility of legislation and of the impossibility of improving the law through conscious effort. The law was thought of as evolving in a necessary course through an inherent power of the idea of freedom to unfold or realize itself. It had moved and must continue to move away from institutions and rules and doctrines in which one's legal rights and duties were consequences of a condition in which he found himself, toward institutions and rules and doctrines in which rights flow from being a conscious, free willing individual and legal duties are consequences of willed action. We could observe this inevitable movement of the law and trace its orbit. We could not affect it or its course.

Few things have been more irritating to the lay public in a time calling for legal growth than the attitude of many of the strongest men in the profession to which the historical mode of thought has given rise. Legislation, the layman's reliance for improving the law, they pronounced vain. It sought to make what could only be found.[60] Juristic science they pronounced equally powerless. Judicial decision could not be asked to achieve changes. It must of necessity run along historically fixed lines.[61] Thus legislation framed at the instance of business men and expressing the needs of commerce was obstructed because it extended the idea of negotiability at the expense of what was conceived as a historical principle that no one could transfer more than he had.[62] Such doctrine, happily much less common than it was twenty-five years ago, invited the legislative steam roller, crude projects of recall, and multiplication of administrative tribunals.

Only a few words need be said about positivism. It had little or no effect on judicial decision. Mostly it confirmed the ideas of the historical jurists. So far as it had influence it furthered the characteristic juristic pessimism of the end of the last century.

Reviewing the theories of judicial decision current in the last century, it will be seen that we began with a creative theory which was used to make an American common law, chiefly of English materials, but with much and effective use of comparative law and not a little translating into legal precepts of the political and social ideas of the new world. As the constructive work proceeded, the creative theory changed in all but name. Later it became a stabilizing factor, and still later, where it lingered at the end of the century, it was a force for obstruction. Its place was taken by analytical and historical theories which assumed that the grounds of judicial decision of causes were preexistent in their entirety as legal precepts, that the process of ascertaining them for a given case was mechanical, that the process of applying them was likewise mechanical and inflexible, and that the judicial process was wholly one of finding preexisting, legally appointed grounds of decision, giving them the preappointed meaning, and applying them with logical exactness. These assumptions by no means accord with the facts. But they represent an ideal of decision to which the last century strove to conform. Moreover they represent an ideal to which for some purposes and in some connections the administration of justice ought to conform. The error was in seeking to extend this ideal, appropriate to property and to commercial transactions, over the whole domain of law. In particular it was a mistake to apply it to conduct and to the conduct of enterprises. Here the demand for individualization is insistent, and has brought about continual inroads upon judicial justice through the setting up of administrative boards and commissions. We should not give up the ideal of the last century wholly. It was a distinct gain for the legal order. But it is not all-sufficient. We must learn how to partition the field. We must seek a theory which will insure the certainty required for the economic order and yet permit the flexibility required for the individual life.

In a developed legal system, when a court decides a case it seeks first to attain justice in that particular cause and second to attain it in accordance with law; on grounds and by a process prescribed in or provided by law. The strict theory of the last century denied the first part of the proposition, conceiving that the judicial function began and ended in applying to an ascertained state of facts a rigidly defined legal formula definitely prescribed as such or exactly deduced from authoritatively prescribed premises. Happily, even in the height of the reign of that theory we did not practise what we preached. Courts could not forget that they were administering justice [63] and the most that such a theory could do was to hamper the judicial instinct to seek a just result. The proceedings of bar associations and the memoirs of our judges written by lawyers are full of evidence of the regard accorded by laymen and lawyer alike to the strong judge who knew how to use the precepts of the law to advance justice in the concrete case. Whenever the exigencies of nineteenth-century theory did not interfere with our real feeling, we honored the magistrate who administered justice, if also according to law.

When justice in the case in hand has been attained as near as may be, and has been attained on grounds and in a manner prescribed by law, the duty of the judge under the classical civil law has been performed. But the Anglo-American judge must do more. At least if he is an appellate judge, he must so decide that his decision will enter into the body of the law as a precedent. He must so decide that his decision, or the grounds thereof, will serve, first, as a measure or pattern of decision of like cases for the future, and, second, as a basis of analogical reasoning in the future for cases for which no exact precedents are at hand. Happily, the bulk of the cases which come before courts on the crowded judicial calendars of today do not call for much care as to this additional duty. They repeat or ring insignificant changes upon familiar states of fact. But each departure, however slight, from states of fact to which settled legal precepts have attached defined legal consequences calls for consideration of the relation of such departure to a just result in the case. Also it calls for consideration of the possible operation of the decision as a precedent or as furnishing an analogy for future cases, and this adds to the burden upon the tribunal. The necessity of weighing not merely the grounds of its decision, but the exact words in which those grounds are expressed, with reference to their possible use in other cases and thus of foreseeing within limits their potential analogical applications, is perhaps the gravest of the burdens involved in the crowded dockets of modern American appellate courts. If it were not for the need of scrupulously careful formulation of their decisions with reference to other cases in the future, our appellate courts could despatch the business that comes before them with less than half of the effort which our system of precedents requires. As it is, one or both of the aspects of the court's function must suffer. Either consideration of the merits of the actual controversy must yield to the need of detailed formulation of a precedent that will not embarrass future decision, or careful formulation must give way to the demand for study of the merits of the case in hand.

In another respect these two sides of the judicial function in Anglo-American law have a reciprocal influence. On the one hand, as the saying is, hard cases make bad law. On the other hand, regard for the stability of the legal order sometimes inclines courts to be callous toward unfortunate results in particular cases. And if a compromise sometimes results, it may very likely give neither a just decision between the parties nor a practicable instrument of justice for the future.

Our reports are full of illustrations of this reciprocal influence of the deciding and the declaring function. More than one general rule, more than one doctrine has been determined or has been directed into a certain course by the hard circumstances of the particular case which first called upon a common-law court to state it or to fix its limits. To put but two instances of arbitrary doctrines with which our case law has since waged a long struggle, consider *Winterbottom* v. *Wright*,[64] which seemed to establish that the general principle of liability for a course of conduct carried on without due care under the circumstances, did not apply to a manufacturer or dealer who negligently put upon the market an article containing an unknown hidden defect, whereby the ultimate purchaser was injured. Consider *Thorogood* v. *Bryan*,[65] which for a time set up an artificial conception of imputed negligence. In each case, when we look narrowly at the cause presented to the court which established the proposition, we discover that there is an element moving behind the logical scene. In each case we struggled painfully for more than half a century to unshackle the law from these decisions and their consequences.[66] In more than one jurisdiction the process is not yet complete.[67] On the other hand, quite as many cases may be found where strong judges have said that the result might be unfortunate in the particular case, but the appointed legal precept or the logical consequences of the applicable precedent must be decisive let the result be what it may.[68] When they reason thus, often they not only sacrifice the interests of the parties to the particular litigation but they extend the potential application of the precept calling for such a result and threaten an ascending series of like sacrifices until the whole has to be overturned.[69]

One cannot understand American case law without bearing in mind the disturbing influence of the facts of particular cases upon the general rule. Nor can he understand American judicial decision without bearing in mind the disturbing effect of the exigencies of our doctrine of precedents upon the disposition of particular cases. At one moment courts are tempted to modify a general rule with reference to appealing circumstances of one case. The next moment fear of impairing a settled rule or of unsettling it by analogy will tempt them to ignore appealing circumstances of another case. If we actually set as much store by single decisions as we purport to do in legal theory, the path of the law would lie in a labyrinth. In truth, our practice has learned to make large allowances for both of these features of decision which are inseparable from a judge-made customary law. Out of the struggle to decide the particular case justly and yet according to law, while at the same time furnishing, or contributing to furnish, a guide for judicial decision hereafter, there comes in time a logically sound and practically workable principle derived from judicial experience of many causes. In the meantime there has been sacrifice of the claims of particular litigants and sacrifice of certainty and order in the law as decision has fluctuated between regard to the one or to the other of the two sides of the judge's duty.

In these considerations lies the explanation of what American lawyers find so hard to understand, namely, how civil-law tribunals, which decide the particular case without settling or attempting to settle any general point of law, merely determining that controversy for those parties on general legal grounds found for that case, can act on such a theory consistently with the general security. In fact their decisions are much more consistent and ours are much less consistent than they appear respectively in theory. Probably about the same degree of certainty is attained in practice in each system.[70] If our results were as rigid or theirs as loose as the respective theories taken at face value indicate, neither system would be tolerable under the conditions of today. Permanent judicial tribunals manned by trained lawyers are sure to follow their own decisions and the decisions of other like tribunals to the extent of being guided by experience and adhering to precepts which have approved themselves in experience. Tribunals set up to administer justice are no less sure to seek and to achieve just results between the parties in spite of theories which call upon them to subordinate such results to formulation of general rules on the basis of the facts of the cases before them.

Our chief lawmaking agency is judicial empiricism.[71] It is the judicial search for the workable legal precept, for the principle which is fruitful of good results in giving satisfactory grounds of decision of actual cases; for the legal conception into which the facts of actual controversies may be fitted with results which accord with justice between the parties to concrete litigations. It is a process of trial and error with all the advantages and disadvantages of such a process.

But what is to guide this judicial search for the law through trial and error? What is to hold down this judicial experimenting with tentative legal propositions in the endeavor to find the practicable precept and to define it by inclusion and exclusion through experience? What is to confine the process within limits compatible with the general security? In the past it has been governed and its path has been defined by ideals of the end of law and of the legal and social order, and such ideals must be our reliance today and tomorrow. But if the work is to be well done, we must be conscious that these ideals are invoked, of the purpose for which they are invoked, and of their paramount importance as maintaining the general security as against rash experimentation and wilful giving rein to personal inclinations. Our theory of judicial decision must recognize what actually takes place and why, and must endeavor to give a rational account of it. But it must also give a rational account of the check upon the process upon which we must rely for safeguarding the general security, and enable us to make that check the most effective for that purpose and yet the least obstructive of legal growth and of individualization of decision that may be. To do this it must give us a picture of the end of law and of the legal and social order adequate to those demands.

This is not the place to discuss what that picture may be or should be.[72] It is enough to say that the legal order has always been and is a system of practical compromises between conflicting and overlapping human claims or wants or desires in which the continual pressure of these claims and of the claims involved in civilized social life has compelled lawmakers and judges and administrators to seek to satisfy the most of the scheme of claims as a whole with the least sacrifice.

On other occasions I have suggested a partition of the field of the legal order between legislation and common law and between judicial justice and administrative justice. This is too large a subject for discussion in the present connection. But it is worth noticing that our theories of decision have not taken account of the possibility of such a partition. They have insisted on one machine, set up with reference to the work to be done in one field, for all the work to be done in all fields. Our current theory of decision as a simple process of mechanical manipulation had its origin in the strict law which was a system of remedies only, before the system of rights, elaborated in the nineteenth century, had been conceived. Thus our ideas of judicial technique, our theory of that technique, are behind our actual practice which, though hampered by the theory, has yet been obliged to improve itself under the pressure of new claims and demands for recognition and better securing of new interests. Our theory of judicial technique belongs to a stage of legal development which antedates the weapons in the judicial armory of today. On the whole, the judges have done their part better than the jurists and the teachers. They have pushed forward cautiously but with reasonable speed along paths worked out by judicial empiricism, while those who should have put the forward movement in the order of reason and should have furnished ideal plans of the forward path, have urged pseudo-scientific reasons why the judges should stand fast and have preached that progress would spontaneously achieve itself.

[1] *E.g.* in Pennsylvania, David Lloyd, William Allen, and Benjamin Chew on the bench, and Andrew Hamilton, Tench Francis, Thomas McKeen, Edward Shippen, George Read, Jared Ingersoll, Alexander J. Dallas, Jasper Yeates at the bar; in Maryland, Daniel Dulaney the Younger; in Virginia, William Bird of Westover, Sir John Randolph, Stevens Thomson, John Ambler, Peyton Randolph, John Randolph; in North Carolina, James Iredell; in South Carolina, John Rutledge, Thomas Hayward, Thomas Lynch, Jr., John Laurens, John Julian Pringle, Edward Rutledge, Charles Cotesworth Pinckney, Thomas Pinckney, William H. Gibbes, Hugh Rutledge.

It will be noticed that in Pennsylvania and Virginia, states in which the influence of the bar was conspicuous in the formative era, in which also lawyers were trained by the apprentice system to go to other states and train students in their offices to hand down their teaching in those new jurisdictions, the English-trained leaders were numerous. The list of English-trained lawyers in colonial and eighteenth-century America includes many of the great names in the beginnings of our law.

[2] For example, the traditional attitude of our American law toward corporations, thinking of them not as modern business devices but in terms of a medieval jealousy of ecclesiastical and municipal corporations (see Machen, Do Incorporation Laws Allow Sufficient Freedom to Commercial Enterprize? [1909] 14 Transactions, Maryland State Bar Assn. 78; People *v.* Shedd, 241 Ill., 155); the traditional attitude of equity toward directors of corporations, largely out of touch with the ideas of businessmen and leaders of finance and industry (Strong *v.* Repide, 213 U. S. 419; McClure *v.* Law, 161 N. Y. 78; General Rubber Co. *v.* Benedict, 215 N. Y. 18; Commonwealth Title & Trust Co. *v.* Seltzer, 227 Pa. St. 410; Oliver *v.* Oliver, 118 Ga. 362; 3 Pomeroy, Equity Jurisprudence [3 ed. 1905], § 1090; 4 Thompson, Corporations [2 ed. 1909], §§ 403–404); the professional distrust of the Massachusetts business trust (see Warren, Corporate Advantages without Incorporation, 719 ff.); the cautious judicial attitude in New York as to a further power of growth in the Law Merchant (President and Directors of the Manhattan Co. *v.* Morgan, 242 N. Y. 38); the obstinate resistance of the traditional law of partnership to the ideas and convenience of the business world (see Crane, Uniform Partnership Act — a Criticism, 28 Harvard Law Rev. 762).

[3] For example, although the Supreme Court of the United States (Van Ness *v.* Packard, 2 Pet. 137) questioned whether the common-law doctrine as to agricultural fixtures was applicable to the conditions of this country, the New York Court of Appeals adhered to the doctrine as a general proposition in Ombony *v.* Jones, 19 N. Y. 234, and it was announced in North Carolina as law in Overman *v.* Sasser, 107 N. C. 432, citing a number of prior decisions in that state.

[4] See Pound, The Spirit of the Common Law, 1–6.

[5] See Chase, Lemuel Shaw.

[6] See Roberts, Memoirs of John Bannister Gibson.

[7] See Graham, Life and Character of Thomas Ruffin.

[8] 4 Met. (Mass.) 49.

[9] See Pound, Interpretations of Legal History, 109–111; Pound, Fifty Years of Jurisprudence, 51 Harvard Law Rev. 777, 777–779. If class self-interest explains the refusal to extend the operation of *respondeat superior*, it should also explain judicial limitation by that doctrine of the principle that liability flows from fault. But this would prove too much. The Marxian economic interpretation requires us to look only at one side of what is to be explained.

[10] 4 Met. (Mass.) 111.

[11] Nelles, Commonwealth *v.* Hunt, 32 Columbia Law Rev. 1128, 1151.

[12] *Id.* 1161.

[13] Davis, History of the Judiciary in Massachusetts, Introductory Chapter, p. v.

[14] *Id.* 188.

[15] *Id.* 189.

[16] *Id.* 189–90. The epithet is quoted from Nelles, *ubi supra*, 1161.

[17] Interpretations of Legal History, 105–109.

[18] See Manson, The Builders of Our Law, 258.

[19] Bohlen, The Rule in Rylands *v.* Fletcher, 59 Univ. of Pa. Law Rev. 298, 318–320.

[20] Shipley *v.* Associates, 106 Mass. 194; Cahill *v.* Eastman, 18 Minn. 324; Defiance Water Co. *v.* Olinger, 54 Ohio St. 532; Weaver *v.* Thurmond, 68 W. Va. 530; French *v.* Mfg. Co., 173 Mo. App. 220, 227; Texas R. Co. *v.* Frazer (Texas Court of Civil Appeals), 182 S. W. 1161.

[21] Brown *v.* Collins, 53 N. H. 422; Losee *v.* Buchanan, 51 N. Y. 476; Marshall *v.* Welwood, 38 N. J. Law, 339; Penn. Coal Co. *v.* Sanderson, 113 Pa. St. 136; Judson *v.* Giant Powder Co., 107 Cal. 549; Owensboro *v.* Knox, 116 Ky. 451; Lake Shore R. Co. *v.* Chicago R. Co., 48 Ind. App. 584.

[22] Paine *v.* Meller, 6 Vesey Jr., 349.

[23] Columbian Co. *v.* Lawrence, 2 Pet. 25, 47; Osborn *v.* Nicholson, 13 Wall. 654, 660.

[24] Willis *v.* Wozencraft, 22 Cal. 607; Phinizy *v.* Guernsey, 111 Ga. 346; Gammon *v.* Blaisdell, 45 Kan. 221; Cottingham *v.* Fireman's Co., 90 Ky. 301; Skinner *v.* Houghton, 92 Md. 68; Walker *v.* Owen, 79 Mo. 563; Franklin Co. *v.* Martin, 40 N. J. Eq. 568; Sewell *v.* Underhill, 197 N. Y. 168; Gilbert *v.* Port, 28 Ohio St. 276; Dunn *v.* Yakish, 10 Okl. 388; Elliott *v.* Ashland Co., 117 Pa. St. 460; Brakhage *v.* Tracy, 13 S. Dak. 343.

[25] Thompson *v.* Gould, 20 Pick. 134.

[26] Cutliffe *v.* McAnally, 88 Ala. 507; Davidson *v.* Hawkeye Co., 71 Ia. 532; Gould *v.* March, 70 Me. 288; Bautz *v.* Kuhworth, 1 Mont. 133; Wilson *v.* Clark, 60 N. H. 352; Elmore *v.* Russell, 88 Ore. 509. The Uniform Vendor and Purchaser Act approved by the National Conference of Commissioners on Uniform State Laws in 1935, adopts a compromise rejecting both rules and proposing to make possession at the time of loss the criterion, Transactions of the National Conference of Commissioners on Uniform State Laws, 1935, 139, adopted with some change by New York Laws, 1936, chap. 731. One can easily explain this compromise on grounds of doctrinal history, where any other explanation is quite impossible.

[27] See Williston, The Risk of Loss after an Executory Contract of Sale in the Common Law, 9 Harvard Law Rev. 106, 111–130; Keener, The Burden of Loss as an Incident of the Right to the Specific Performance of a Contract, 1 Columbia Law Rev. 1.

[28] Rev. Stat. Ills. 1845, chap. 73, §§ 2–3.

[29] See Pound, The Judicial Office in America, 10 Boston Univ. Law Rev. 125.

[30] Davis, History of the Judiciary of Massachusetts, 86–103.

[31] Whitehead, The Supreme Court of New Jersey, 3 Green Bag, 401, 402–405.

[32] Warren, History of the American Bar, 134–135.

[33] Edwards, The Supreme Court of Rhode Island, 2 Green Bag, 525, 531–532.

[34] Wallace, The Reporters, 4 ed., 561–591.

[35] Geist des römischen Rechts, 2 ed., III, 11.

[36] See Pound, The Ideal Element in American Judicial Decision, 45 Harvard Law Rev. 136, 142–144, 147.

[37] See cases cited *ibid.* 139–140.

[38] Ogden *v.* Saunders, 12 Wheat. 213, 353–354.

[39] See Pound, Mechanical Jurisprudence, 8 Columbia Law Rev. 605.

[40] See Schulz, Prinzipien des römischen Rechts, 151–161; Windscheid, Pandekten, I, § 44; Sohm, Institutionen Geschichte und System des römischen Rechts (17 ed. by Mitteis and Wenger), § 18, pp. 105–107, § 115, III, pp. 688–689.

[41] Doctor and Student, Dial. II, chap. 24; Pound, Consideration in Equity, Wigmore Celebration Legal Essays, 435. I have discussed this more fully in Law and Morals, 34–42.

[42] Kant, Metaphysische Anfangsgründe der Rechtslehre, 2 ed. 1798; Bentham, Principles of Morals and Legislation, 1780; Savigny, Vom Beruf unsrer Zeit für Gesetzgebung und Rechtswissenschaft, 1814, had definitely ushered in the modes of juristic thought which were to prevail in the nineteenth century.

[43] See Pound, The Spirit of the Common Law, lect. 4.

[44] Kent, Memoirs of Chancellor Kent, 112, 117. See, for example, 1 Story, Equity Jurisprudence, §§ 139–140, 186, 192–203.

[45] Van Ness *v.* Pacard, 2 Pet. 137.

[46] Chase, J. in Calder *v.* Bull, 3 Dall. 386, 388–89; Terrett *v.* Taylor, 9 Cranch 43, 50–51; Wilkinson *v.* Leland, 2 Pet. 627, 658; St. Louis *v.* The Ferry Co., 11 Wall. 423, 429; Field, J. in Slaughter House Cases, 16 Wall, 36, 95; Miller, J. in Loan Ass'n *v.* Topeka, 20 Wall. 655, 663–664;

Monongahela Navigation Co. *v.* United States, 148 U. S. 312, 324; Chicago, B. & Q. R. R. *v.* Chicago, 166 U. S. 226, 235–241; Holden *v.* Hardy, 169 U. S. 366, 389; Madisonville Traction Co. *v.* St. Bernard Mining Co., 196 U. S. 239, 251–252; In re Dorsey, 7 Port. (Ala.) 293, 377–378; Jeffers *v.* Fair, 33 Ga. 347, 367; Regents of the University of Maryland *v.* Williams, 9 Gill & J. 365, 408–409; State *v.* Barker, 116 Iowa 96, 105; State *v.* Nemaha County, 7 Kan. 542, 555–556; Holden *v.* James, 11 Mass. 396, 405; Commonwealth *v.* Perry, 155 Mass. 117, 121; White *v.* White, 5 Barb. 474, 484–485; Benson *v.* Mayor, 10 Barb. (N. Y.) 223, 245; Nunnemacher *v.* State, 129 Wis. 190, 197–202. In Jeffers *v.* Fair, this ideal was made to read an extreme doctrine of states' rights into the Confederate constitution, there being no express language in the instrument on the point in question.

[47] Holden *v.* James, 11 Mass. 396, 405; Sohier *v.* Mass. Gen. Hospital, 3 Cush. (Mass.) 483, 493; Gillilan *v.* Gillilan, 278 Mo. 99, 111–113; State *v.* Moores, 55 Neb. 480, 490. In Gillilan *v.* Gillilan primogeniture in estates tail was held "contrary to the theory on which this and other commonwealths were built." The statute provided that the remainder should pass in fee simple absolute to the person "to whom the estate tail would on the death of the first grantee, devisee or donee in tail first pass according to the course of the common law" (278 Mo. 112). In Massachusetts the same provision had been held to adopt primogeniture, giving the first taker an estate for life and the common-law heir in tail a fee simple.

[48] Adair *v.* United States, 208 U. S. 161, 175; Godcharles *v.* Wigeman, 113 Pa. St. 431; State *v.* Haun, 61 Kan. 146, 162; State *v.* Fire Creek Coal & Coke Co., 33 W. Va. 188, 190; Frorer *v.* People, 141 Ill. 171, 186; Ritchie *v.* People, 155 Ill. 99, 111; State *v.* Goodwill, 33 W. Va. 179, 186; Braceville Coal Co. *v.* People, 147 Ill. 66, 74.

[49] "A command proceeding from the supreme political au-

thority of a state and addressed to the persons who are the subjects of that authority." Amos, Science of Law, 48 (1874). "The will of the state concerning the civic conduct of those under its authority." Woodrow Wilson, The State, § 1415 (1898).

[50] See Maine, Early History of Institutions, 7 ed., 362–365; Carter, Law: Its Origin, Growth and Function, 13–25, 115–136.

[51] See Vinogradoff, Historical Jurisprudence, I, 128–135.

[52] Pomeroy, Introduction to Municipal Law, 2 ed., §§ 301–309 (1883).

[53] Austin, Jurisprudence, 3 ed., I, 37, II, 676, 682; Markby, Elements of Law, 6 ed., §§ 25–30.

[54] Wayman *v.* Southard, 10 Wheat. 1, 42, 50; Bank of United States *v.* Halstead, 10 Wheat. 51, 61; Beers *v.* Horton, 9 Pet. 329, 358; Baldwin, J. in Norwalk Street Railway Co.'s Appeal, 69 Conn. 576, 605–607.

[55] Philosophically this goes back to Kant's theory of the legal order as a reconciling of wills according to a common rule of freedom. Metaphysische Anfangsgründe der Rechtslehre, 27.

[56] Anson, Principles of the English Law of Contract, §§ 2–5; Wald's Pollock on Contracts, 1–5. See Holmes, Common Law, lect. 5.

[57] For example, the way in which liability in case of continuing carriers was treated on the basis of bargain rather than of duty to provide facilities. Gray *v.* Jackson, 51 N. H. 9; Michigan C. R. Co. *v.* Myrick, 107 U. S. 102; Washburn *v.* P. & W. R. Co., 113 Mass. 490; Jennings *v.* Grand Trunk R. Co., 127 N. Y. 438. Cf. the legislative rule on this subject: Act of June 29, 1906, c. 3591, § 7, 34 St. L. 584, 595; Atlantic Coast Line *v.* The Riverside Mills, 219 U. S. 186, 197–207. See also the doctrine that no demurrage may be charged except in maritime law unless by virtue of contract, custom, or statute. Chicago & N. W. R. Co. *v.* Jenkins, 103

Ill. 588. From a modern standpoint this is now held to be a reasonable incident of the relation. Schumacher *v.* Chicago R. Co., 207 Ill. 199, 212; Miller *v.* Ga. R. Co., 88 Ga. 563; Swan *v.* Louisville & N. R. Co., 106 Tenn. 229; Baltimore & Ohio R. Co. *v.* Luella Coal Co., 74 West Va. 289. Cf. also the inability of the courts to distinguish between a horse and wagon carrier giving a neighbor a lift between two villages or gratuitously carrying as passenger, and a chartered railroad corporation distributing passes about the community or making special rates for favorite shippers. Fitchburg R. Co. *v.* Gage, 12 Gray 393, 398–399; Great Western R. Co. *v.* Sutton, 4 Eng. & Irish App. 226, 227; Johnson *v.* Pensacola R. Co., 16 Fla. 623, 667; Ex parte Benson, 18 S. C. 38, 43. The cases are collected in 2 Wyman, Public Service Corporations, § 1282. See Interstate Commerce Commission *v.* Baltimore & Ohio R. Co., 145 U. S. 263, 275. Note also how the law of public service companies was sought to be deduced from the theory of a legal transaction, either on the basis of a transaction of professing a public employment, which darkened counsel in the cases as to use of trains by express companies — cf. The D. R. Morris, 11 Blatchford 232; Pfister *v.* Central Pac. R. Co., 70 Calif. 169; Blank *v.* Ill. C. R. Co., 80 Ill. App. 475; Sargent *v.* Boston & Lowell R. Co., 115 Mass. 416; with The Express Cases, 117 Mass. 1, State *v.* Missouri Pac. R. Co., 241 Mo. 117; Sandford *v.* C. W. & E. R. Co., 24 Pa. St. 378; McDuffee *v.* Portland and Rochester R. R., 52 N. H. 430 — or on the basis of a legal transaction of dedication to a public use, as to which see Waite, C. J. in Munn *v.* Illinois, 94 U. S. 113, 126; and cf. Alvey, C. J. in Chesapeake and P. Tel. Co. *v.* Baltimore and Ohio Tel. Co., 66 Md. 399, 414; note also how questions as to the duties of companies chartered to operate railroads were beclouded by arguments as to what was professed by a person in the habit of hauling in his cart from the wharf to country storekeepers in the interior; Kansas Pacific Ry. Co. *v.* Nichols, Kennedy & Co., 9 Kansas

235, 253. Note the argument of counsel, pages 239–240, and the situation in Tunnel *v.* Pettijohn, 2 Harr. (Del.) 48; cf. Faucher *v.* Wilson, 68 N. H. 338 with Jackson *v.* Hurlbut, 158 N. Y. 34.

[58] Thayer, Liability without Fault, 29 Harvard Law Rev. 801; Smith, Tort and Absolute Liability, 30 *id.* 241, 319, 409; Isaacs, Fault and Liability, 31 Harvard Law Rev. 954.

[59] "The doctrine is a stubborn archaism." Pollock, Torts, 11 ed. 501, note *y*. "In every case of the kind which has been reported since Rylands *v.* Fletcher, that is, during the last twenty-five years, there has been a manifest inclination to discover something in the facts which took the case out of the rule. . . . There are some authorities which are followed and developed in the spirit, which become the starting point of new chapters of the law; there are others that are followed in the letter and become slowly but surely choked and crippled by exceptions." Pollock, The Law of Fraud in British India, 53–54 (1894). See also Salmond, Torts, 4 ed., 233, arguing that the doctrine has no application if no one has been negligent. But the English courts have refused to limit the doctrine to adjacent freeholders and have extended it to new situations of fact. Charing Cross Electricity Supply Co. *v.* Hydraulic Power Co., [1914] 3 K. B. 772, 779, 785; Musgrove *v.* Pandelis, [1919] 2 K. B. 43. Likewise absolute liability of those who maintain dangerous animals, and other trespassing animals, supposed to have been disappearing anomalies, have shown unusual vitality. Liability for dangerous animals has been unheld to the very verge in the case of an animal wrongfully turned loose by an intermeddler. Baker *v.* Snell, [1908] 2 K. B. 352, 355. Also this liability has been applied to collateral consequences of a trespass. Theyer *v.* Purnell, [1918] 2 K. B. 333. More recently equity has applied Rylands *v.* Fletcher by analogy to a situation very like the American automobile tourist camp. Attorney-General *v.* Corke, [1933] 1 Ch. 89. The dogma of no liability without fault led

American courts a generation ago to hold workmen's compensation acts unconstitutional because legislative imposition of such liability was not due process of law. Ives *v.* South Buffalo R. Co., 201 N. Y. 271, 285, 287, 293, 295. Yet the principle of liability only as a corollary of fault was never equal to explaining the whole field of liability for tort in New York which carried the doctrine furthest and applied it most consistently. Thus in New York the owner was held "bound at his peril" to keep his cattle at home. R. Co. *v.* Munger, 5 Denio 255, 267. An infant too young to have fault imputed to it was none the less liable in tort. Bullock *v.* Babcock, 3 Wend. 391. A lunatic who would not be responsible criminally was liable in tort. Williams *v.* Hays, 143 N. Y. 442. And there was liability for injuries to the person by blasting operations although there was no negligence. Sullivan *v.* Dunham, 161 N. Y. 290.

[60] Carter, Law: Its Origin, Growth and Function, lect. 9.

[61] Note in 8 Michigan Law Rev. 315; Note in 4 Harvard Law Rev. 384, 395; Supervisors *v.* Decker, 30 Wis. 624, 626–627, 629–630.

[62] Burdick, A Revival of Codification, 10 Columbia Law Rev. 118, 123, 125–126.

[63] Dillon, Laws and Jurisprudence of England and America, 17–18.

[64] 10 M. & W. 109 (1842).

[65] 8 C. B. 115 (1849).

[66] The doctrine of Winterbottom *v.* Wright was not seriously shaken till MacPherson *v.* Buick Motor Co., 217 N. Y. 382 (1916). The doctrine of Thorogood *v.* Bryan was rejected for the United States in Little *v.* Hackett, 116 U. S. 366 (1885) and for England in The Bernina, 12 P. Div. 58 (1887), affirmed in Mills *v.* Armstrong, 13 App. Cas. 1.

[67] As to the doctrine of Winterbottom *v.* Wright, see McAllister (Donaghue) *v.* Stevenson, [1932] A. C. 562; Grant *v.* Australian Knitting Mills, [1936] A. C. 85; Pollock,

The Snail in the Bottle, and Thereafter, 49 Law Quarterly Rev. 22. As to the doctrine of Thorogood *v.* Bryan, see American Law Institute, Restatement of the Law of Torts, II, § 491.

[68] See Willoughby, The Distinctions and Anomalies Arising out of the Equitable Doctrine of the Legal Estate, 71–72.

[69] "I have known judges, bred in the world of legal studies, who delighted in nothing so much as in a strong decision. Now a strong decision is a decision opposed to common sense and common convenience. . . . A great part of the law made by judges consists of strong decisions, and as one strong decision is a precedent for another a little stronger the law at last, on some matters, becomes such a nuisance that equity intervenes or an Act of Parliament must be passed to sweep the whole away." Erle, C. J. *ex rel.* Senior, Conversations with Distinguished Persons, 1880 ed., 314.

[70] See Goodhart, Precedent in English and Continental Law (1934), and my review, 48 Harvard Law Rev. 863.

[71] I have discussed this at length in The Spirit of the Common Law, lect. 7.

[72] See Pound, How Far Are We Attaining a New Measure of Values in Twentieth-Century Juristic Thought, 42 West Virginia Law Quarterly, 81.

IV

DOCTRINAL WRITING

NO truthful account of the development of American law in the nineteenth century can ignore the part played by text writers. While in form our law is chiefly the work of judges, in great part judges simply put the guinea stamp of the state's authority upon propositions which they found worked out for them in advance. Their creative work was often a work of intelligent selection. In this respect, as also in the part played by law teachers, American law is closer to the civil law than to the English common law. Yet doctrinal writing played in every way a very much greater part in the growth of the common law to its maturity in the last century than our juristic theory admits. Bentham says that law is made by "Judge and Company," meaning that counsel, by their argument, have much to do with judicial finding and shaping of the law. Certainly the most creative of judges have not made legal precepts out of their own minds, nor have they been inspired wholly by "authority." Text books have had and still have much influence. In the formative era of American law this influence was often controlling.

Indeed, the nineteenth-century text writers did much more for English law at home than appears upon the surface. Chief Baron Pollock is reported to have said that he "read no treatises" but "referred to them as collecting the authorities."[1] However, the systematic collection of the authorities in the hands of a skillful writer involves suggestive interpretation of them and the way in which they are set forth may be and often was more than a mere indexing of them. It is true the English have or had some strict rules as to citation. The writer to be cited must have been or have become a judge, and the living were not to be cited.[2] Thus Byles on Bills (1829), Sugden on Vendor and Purchaser (1805) and Sugden on Powers (1808) could be cited for what had been written before the authors went upon the bench. So with Lindley on Partnership (1863) and later its outgrowth Lindley on the Law of Companies. But one would deceive himself much if he thought that Jarman on Wills (1844) or Lewin on Trusts (1837) or Preston on Estates (1820) did no more than serve as collections of the authorities. Moreover, at a later date, the books from which English law students learned their law succeeded more than once in bringing into English judicial decision and thence into the American books ideas from the nineteenth-century Pandectists — sometimes ideas which were not as happy as they seemed.

We had no such rules as to citation in America. Here the judicial use of text books was general and avowed and not always discriminating.

It is curious that Louisiana, where there was a civil-law tradition, did not contribute any notable texts to the doctrinal literature of American law, while our common-law jurisdictions, where the tradition attributed little weight to treatises, developed treatises which had so wide an influence. But it costs money to publish law text books. In practice such books could not be published unless there was much more than a local market. Louisiana was too restricted a field and Louisiana law was too foreign to that of the rest of the land to make it profitable for the Louisiana lawyer to essay to write a general treatise of the first order.

American text writing as a significant force in our legal development begins in 1816 with Reeve's, Baron and Feme. Down to the Civil War the list of text books which went far to shape the law for us is impressive: Kent's Commentaries (1826–1830); Gould on Pleading (1832); Story on Bailments (1832), on the Constitution (1833), on the Conflict of Laws (1834), on Equity Jurisprudence (1836), on Equity Pleading (1838), on Agency (1839), on Partnership (1841), on Bills of Exchange (1843), on Promissory Notes (1845); Wheaton on International Law (1836); Greenleaf on Evidence (1842–1853); Wharton on Criminal Law (1846); Sedgwick on Damages (1847) and on Interpretation of Statutory and Constitutional Law (1857); Rawle on Covenants for Title (1852); Bishop on Marriage and Divorce (1852) and on Criminal Law (1856–1858); Parsons on Contracts (1853–1855); Washburn on Real Property (1860–1862). All of these went through many editions. They were standard to the end of the century, some well into the present century, and some are standard even today. So much were they used by the profession and by the courts that an indignant practitioner is said to have demanded of a court as to one of them whether there was any statute making it an authority.[8]

From the Civil War to the end of the century, Cooley's Constitutional Limitations (1868), Dillon on Municipal Corporations (1872) and Pomeroy's Equity Jurisprudence (1881–1883) exhaust the list of those which can stand with the great texts of the formative era. But by this time our case law had reached maturity and for a time the need of writings such as those of the earlier period had ceased.

Let us note more in detail what these doctrinal treatises of the fore part of the century were able to bring about. The most important of them were the work of law teachers — Kent, Gould, Story, Greenleaf, Parsons, and Washburn. Few books by law teachers speak from the date upon the title page. The teacher transmits in large part a new version of what he was taught. When after some years of teaching he puts his teachings in print, they are likely to be in a mold of the thought of a generation before. Thus, Blackstone's Commentaries, with a date of 1765, often speak rather from the law of 1700. One would not suspect from Blackstone's pages the work of Hardwicke in equity nor the development in the law of contracts which had gone on for two generations before.[4] Again, Mr. Carter's law school lectures, published in 1907 in his well known book "Law: Its Origin, Growth, and Function," speak not from the twentieth century but from the last quarter of the nineteenth century.[5] Certainly their thought cannot be put later than 1890, the date of his address, "The Ideal and the Actual in Law," in which the leading ideas of the lectures are already fully developed. In like manner, Timothy Walker wrote in 1833, in deprecation of the doctrine that the common law was not in force where not applicable to American conditions, in the spirit of a generation before when men were full of faith in legislatures and felt that courts should not be permitted to pass upon such questions.[6] In a time when the bench, with the guidance of text writers, was about to take definitely the lead in making over the received English law, he wrote as if the beginnings of that leadership were to be deprecated. Men had felt a generation before that there was need of casting off much in the received English materials which was not adapted to American society or in accord with American ideals. But at the same time they felt the impairment of stability involved in a doctrine that no rule of law was established, as something to which the legal adviser might tie, until its applicability to American conditions had been tried and determined in the local court of last resort. They were dissatisfied with much in the inherited or received legal materials. They desired great changes. Yet they saw the unsettling implications of far-reaching change and were no less dissatisfied with the uncertainties which the pressure for change had provided. Hence, they looked to legislation as the agency of change. Instead, the stabilizing agency of change proved to be text writing, and, indeed, text writing by teachers. Moreover, for once the teacher text writers spoke from their own time. The text writer of our formative era had to speak from the date of his book. He had to expound a law which he learned as he went along in expounding it.

Not only were these books the product of teaching, they became and remained the basis of law teaching down to the present century.[7] Thus, they became immediately the basis of a taught tradition and so got quickly a real even if not a theoretical authority. Maitland tells us that taught law is tough law.[8] That is, it is enduring. That these books could at the same time serve practitioner and teacher insured their triumph.

First, they fixed the reception of the common law for all but one of our jurisdictions. This was still in doubt at the end of the first third of the last century. It was never in doubt thereafter.

Eighteenth-century law and eighteenth-century thinking were passing off the stage in the United States. Kent had given natural law a historical content and was shifting the theoretical basis of positive law from natural law to history, from reason to experience.[9] In Story on the Constitution, published in 1833, the transition is complete from an eighteenth-century contract basis of rights and contract basis of government to a historical basis, confirmed by a constitution which declares natural rights with a historical content.[10] The age of reason was coming to an end. The age of history had begun.

Where the eighteenth century had ignored the legal past and had felt able to make all things legal anew, out of whole cloth, by sheer reason, the nineteenth century was putting its faith in historical continuity.

One feature of this feeling for historical continuity was to bring to an end the agitation to supplant the common law as the basis of American legal systems. Many things had operated to retard a complete and final reception of the English common law, not the least the example of the French Civil Code, the enthusiasm for things French following the Revolution and in the era of Jeffersonian democracy, and the natural-law idea that a code could be drafted independent of the historical materials of the law and on a basis of pure reason. It is significant that Walker's American Law (1837) contains a vigorous argument for codification which is retained in later editions down to 1895.[11] In 1833 it was still not wholly settled that we should receive the common law in every state but one, and largely in that state. But Story had begun to write and under his decisive influence the struggle was substantially at an end.

Blackstone and Kent, it is true, had prepared the way, Blackstone especially being taken for an authoritative statement of the law we had received. But they did not and could not go sufficiently into detail for the everyday purposes of the courts. The courts had to turn to what they could find elsewhere, particularly as there were still few American reports. Pothier on Obligations had been translated by François Xavier Martin in 1802, but the translation was not generally accessible.[12] Pothier's treatise on Sales was translated in 1839.[13] Domat had been translated in 1720 and there was a second edition in 1737. These were English. There was an American edition in 1850.[14] Pothier's treatise on partnership was not translated till 1854.[15] It will be seen that most of these translations came too late. Between 1832 and 1845 Story had covered the whole field of commercial law as well as constitutional law and equity with books which at once came into general use.

In the meantime, however, the exigencies of commercial law, on which there was no useful material in Blackstone, had led to an increasing resort by the courts to the civilian treatises. Kent's Commentaries did not appear till 1826–1830. For over a generation after the Revolution the civilians had this field to themselves. In the first volume of Johnson's Reports, reporting decisions of the Supreme Court of New York and of the Court of Errors and Appeals of New York during the year 1806, Pothier is cited four times, Emerigon five times, Valin three times, Casaregis twice, and Azuni once.[16] In seventh Johnson (1810–1811) Pothier is cited three times, Huberus twice, Emerigon once, Justinian's Code once, and the French Civil Code once.[17]

From commercial law this tendency to rely upon the civilians spread to the private law generally. Thus, in the first volume of Johnson's reports in a case involving the conflict of laws, counsel for the plaintiff cited Pothier, counsel for the defendant cited Huberus, Erskine's Institutes of the Law of Scotland, and Justinian's Institutes, and the court followed Pothier.[18] In other cases civilians are cited on common-law questions such as damages on a covenant for title,[19] original acquisition of title to property,[20] rights as between owners in common, and quasi contract.[21] The phenomenon is particularly noticeable in New York because that was pre-eminently a commercial jurisdiction. But examples might be drawn, though to a less extent, from the whole country. Indeed, as late as 1871, when Langdell, trained under Parsons in the fifties, wished to present materials for study of the law as to the formation of a simple contract, he included a discussion by Merlin.[22]

As I have said in another connection, in effect the result was a conception of an ideal of comparative law as declaratory of natural law, a conception which is especially marked in the writings and judgments of Kent and Story. It was not merely creative, it made for stability and gave direction both to judicial decision and to doctrinal writing. It was the most efficient of the instruments by which the great text writers of the formative era were able to bring it about that the English common law should be the basis of the law in all but one of the United States.

But it was not merely that for more than a generation after the Revolution there were no English treatises of consequence on commercial law. When the lawyer or judge of that time sought detailed information as to English law, he had to go to Coke's Institutes, Hale's Tracts and Pleas of the Crown, precedents of pleading, and alphabetically arranged abridgments. Not unnaturally those who could read them turned with delight to the treatises on the civil and commercial law of Continental Europe. When they compared the order and system and rational modernity of the civilian treatises with the disorder and alphabetical arrangement and scholastic medievalism of the English books of the time, they were led to think much worse of English law and much better of the law of Continental Europe than the facts warranted. The high estimate of the civil law which was formed in that period lingered in this country till the end of the third quarter of the last century. But it lingered only as a traditional admiration of something not really understood. Henry Adams going to Germany in the late fifties to study the civil law is one of the last cases of what might have been such a phenomenon as the flow of Scotch students of law to the Dutch universities down to the nineteenth century.[23] As good texts in English appeared in America and few could read the untranslated civilians, the cult of the civil law disappeared.

I suppose a story not unlike the foregoing could be told of the reception of French law in Louisiana and the shaping of your private law chiefly on the basis of the French Civil Code. I suppose very little that had gone on before that code left any permanent mark and that your legal development in your formative period was affected by an influx of common-law ideas and methods and precepts much as the legal development of our common-law jurisdictions was affected by the systematic ideas of the civilians and by civilian doctrines and conceptions. But I must leave this to you who know the story better.

It should be added that, except on commercial law, the great civilian treatises did not deal with the sort of thing which had to be decided in American courts of the formative era. It was hard to find in them the help which the courts and lawyers of the time required. To use them intelligently called for a training and technique quite unknown in English-speaking jurisdictions. As we look at these treatises now, without consulting them under the pressure of cases to be decided at once and with leisure to use them not as books of reference but as systematic expositions of the law as a whole, interdependent in the several parts, and thus to work out their possibilities as their authors intended, we may see that the rich civilian literature of the seventeenth and eighteenth centuries could have been made to yield abundant useful principles and analogies. But the courts needed rules. To perceive the possibilities of finding them by reasoning from the Continental treatises, one had to be a much better civilian than any one could have been at that time — than any one but Kent and Story actually was. Law, as distinguished from laws, is a taught tradition. The civil law was and is an academically taught tradition. There were no faculties of law, trained in and teaching the civil-law tradition, to give vitality to the texts of that law in this country. But if we could not use this legal literature as a whole there was much in it which we could and did use. The genius of the civilians was chiefly employed upon what may be called in a broad sense the law of contractual obligations; upon that part of the law which has to do with recognizing and giving effect to the intention of the parties to legal transactions to create rights and duties; which has to do with the intention implicit in such transactions and the rights and duties annexed to the relations to which they give rise.[24] The side of the law which called for immediate development in the formative era was the very side where the civilians could help, and it was fortunate that there were a few strong judges and well trained, well read doctrinal writers who knew how to avail themselves of that help and make it available for the courts.

In the second place, then, doctrinal writing gave the courts at a critical period what they could take to be authoritative statements of the received common law and so gave judges and legislators something from which to make required new starts. Take for example the Georgia Code of 1860. The part known as the civil code, made up of 1586 sections, is a digest of extracts from the ordinary text books of the common law in use in the United States at the time. It is not a code in the modern sense. But it furnished an authoritative text book of the common law at a time when many questions remained unsettled in that jurisdiction and libraries in which to find the materials for passing upon them were not generally at hand. Such a thing could not have been done without the text books. Indeed, there are gaps in that code exactly where there were gaps in the text book legal literature of the time. Courts not infrequently wrote opinions out of the text books exactly as the Georgia code commission made a code out of them.

Thirdly, the doctrinal writing of the formative era delivered us from the danger of premature crude codification. For there was a very real danger of premature crude codification during the legislative reform movement. Bentham's writings attracted wide attention. The French Civil Code had fascinated many, as it had almost every one abroad. Lay discussions of American law in the first quarter of the nineteenth century abound in demands for an American code. The New York constitution of 1846 provided for a system of codes.[25] Massachusetts had a code commission under legislative authority which made on the whole a favorable report.[26] Georgia adopted a civil code, such as it was, on the eve of the Civil War.[27] California adopted Field's draft codes. In a comparison of abstract systems the common law is at its worst.[28] There was no handy compendium to show to the pioneer with his boundless faith in versatility; to assure him that with it and his common sense he could solve all the legal problems of daily life. The strength of the common law is in its treatment of concrete controversies as the strength of the civil law is in its logical development of abstract conceptions. The latter can be put in much smaller compass than the former and has much more appearance of completeness and certainty. Had such men as Kent and Story allowed their good sense to be overcome by the Continental philosophers of law, whom they undoubtedly admired, the future of American law might have been very different. I doubt if our judges would have been strong enough to withstand the movement for codification. But when the movement culminated in the draft code of David Dudley Field,[29] English law was thoroughly received, well established, and able to resist it.

Fourthly, doctrinal writing preserved unity in our law when its unity was sorely threatened. In the cult of local law which developed in the nineteenth century with the continual setting up of new commonwealths each with independent power to make law by legislation and find it by judicial decision, our American law might have lost its unity. Had it lost its unity the movement for a premature Benthamite code might well have swept the country as the French codes swept over Europe. If the flood of statutes which poured from our legislatures from the beginning had been turned upon a system of purely local rules, as the country became unified economically we should very likely be seeking relief in codes, if we had not done so long ago. An intolerable diversity of local law in a politically and economically unified land has always led to codification.[80] The attempt of the Supreme Court of the United States to preserve unity by its doctrine as to questions of general law[81] could achieve relatively little because the bulk of ordinary questions of private law could not come before that court as fast as they arose in the state courts. What Story the judge could not do, Story the text writer largely accomplished. More than anything else the books of our great nineteenth-century text writers defeated the urge for a code which we were in no condition to frame in our formative era. In Louisiana you had the French Civil Code for a solid foundation. But in jurisdictions which had inherited English law there was no such foundation. There was nothing ripe to be codified. Codification could only come effectively after an era of legal maturity which was still well in the future. A code in the common-law states of nineteenth-century America would have required far longer to develop into a workable body of American law than it took under the leadership of our great doctrinal writers to make such a body of law from the traditional materials. If one doubts this he need only look at the California Code, which has been made to serve chiefly by assuming it to be declaratory of what has been worked out there and elsewhere by judicial experience.[82]

Fifth, doctrinal writing was the chief agency in

saving equity for us as a part of our received system. It was in equity especially that the text writer's method of comparative law was fruitful of good results. Over and above the hostility to all English law there was for historical reasons special hostility to English equity, so that the courts of Pennsylvania did not have equity jurisdiction as such till 1836 [83] nor did the courts of Massachusetts have complete equity jurisdiction till the last quarter of the nineteenth century.[84] Equity has never been popular in America. The Puritan has always opposed it. It acts directly upon the person. It coerces the individual will. It involves discretion in its application to concrete cases and that in the Puritan mind means that a magistrate is over us instead of with us. It means that he may judge by a personal standard instead of by the "standing laws" which the Puritan demanded in the Massachusetts Bill of Rights.[85] He called for a universal and unyielding rule, and it was such things that equity sought to mitigate. Moreover, the pioneer was suspicious of equity because it relieved fools who had made bad bargains, whereas the self-reliant frontiersman felt that fools should be allowed and required to act freely and be held for the consequences of their folly. Nor were the methods and doctrines of equity congenial to our nineteenth-century tribunals. The text writers of the decadence of our law-book writing tried hard to reduce the principles of exercise of the chancellor's discretion to hard and fast rules as to jurisdiction.

Probably the decisive factor in our reception of English equity was Story's Equity Jurisprudence. With much art, whether conscious or unconscious, he made it seem that the precepts established by the decisions of the English Court of Chancery coincided in substance with those of the Roman law as expounded by the civilians and hence were but statements of universal principles of natural law universally accepted in civilized states. If equity had been expounded to American judges and lawyers and students in the dry and technical fashion of the contemporary English treatises, we might have been sorely hampered in the development of American law by a crippled equity. Story's sympathetic exposition of English equity, referring continually to the civilians and to the Roman law, making it appear, untruly as we know now, that the system was essentially Roman and so approved by experience of all men as a body of universal principles of justice, often comparing the development of these principles in England with that upon the Continent to the disadvantage of the latter, and all this in most readable form, with an orderly arrangement and a system which at least improved immeasurably upon what had gone before, was the one thing needed to commend equity to our American courts and to counteract the forces which were working against it.

Lastly, doctrinal writing in the formative era saved us from legislative experimentation at a time when legislatures were not well prepared to deal with the general development of an American private law. What might have happened, if our law had been forced to grow up by legislative empiricism, the New York Code of Civil Procedure, its overgrown mass in the last quarter of the nineteenth century, and the struggles to get away from it and its results in the present generation,[86] warn us abundantly.

In the organizing, systematizing era after the Civil War text writing ceased to be doctrinal writing and became what Chief Baron Pollock said of English text writing, a mere key to the cases. This period was the nadir of American law-book writing. Writers assumed to find a rule for everywhere in a common-law decision anywhere. So far as possible by plausible formulation and consecutive statement they made those independent decisions read like parts of an integrated logically interdependent whole. Where this could not be done, they announced a difference of judicial view, on which they seldom ventured an opinion, for they were stating "the law as it is,"[87] and pointed out the numerical weight of authority in a list of cases in accord and to the contrary, in which very likely New York and Nevada each counted as one. In part, this resulted from the firm basis for judicial decision which had become established in the formative era. The courts could for the most part find what they wanted in the reports. But in part it resulted from the growth of the law-publishing business to large proportions. The exigencies of large-scale publication, with traveling law-book salesmen going from city to city and office to office — a system still in full vigor when I came to the bar in 1890 — called for nationally marketable treatises, and the text book which was the best index to the reports best met that requirement. An orderly presentation of all the cases in the English-speaking world in narrative form, reconciled in illusory appearance at least, so far as the writer's skill would allow, could find a publisher. Criticism of decisions threw doubt upon the proposition that American law, or even the common law, was a body of detailed rules, evidenced by reported cases, in which a decision of an appellate court in any common-law jurisdiction established a rule for every other. The law-publishing business was based upon this postulate. There might at most be cases where a writer could only set forth the "weight of authority" with an appendix of decisions establishing a "minority view." In time such books were superseded by the development of excellent systems of digests, both general and for each state, and of cyclopedias, proceeding on the same presupposition as the mechanical text books, but with a better mechanism.

Let us look more closely at the reasons why, in spite of the common-law tradition and with no formal authority behind them, doctrinal writers were able to become so great a factor in the shaping of American law. One reason was that in our formative era, as a result of our political history, of the tradition of masterful judges under the Stuarts in the time when the colonists emigrated, of the memory of some royal chief justices and judges before the Revolution, and as a legacy of Puritanism, there was general fear of entrusting to judges the power which the common-law polity called for. To some extent the judges of that time did not always have full confidence in themselves, as shown by the rejection of the common-law doctrine as to misdemeanors in the states of the Northwest Territory although the Ordinance of 1787 had made the common law the measure of decision in that domain.[88] If they could not fall back on a statute for a definitely prescribed rule of decision, let them at least use a law book. As late as 1837, Walker argues that there is danger in admitting judicial empiricism as an agency of lawmaking. He says: "Although in theory precedents are binding, yet in point of fact judges do not regard precedents as absolutely imperative like statutes, but rather as lights to aid their discretion and inform their judgment. They sometimes overrule their own prior decisions, and very often the decisions of other courts, in so much that a collection of overruled cases has been published, exceeding a thousand."[39] Obviously the prevalence of such views made for resort to the text books. We can understand why so many courts so often accepted text-book statements of supposed general rules of law.

Then, too, we had before us the example of a growing body of law text writing in England. Hale had begun something of the sort in the seventeenth century.[40] In the eighteenth century there comes to be a marked departure from the alphabetical abridgment or digest type or the discussive-commentary type of law writing which had governed from the Middle Ages to Coke. Of the eighteenth-century texts much cited in America in the fore part of the nineteenth century, we may note Gilbert's treatises (1734–1758), Foster's Crown Law (1762), Fearne's Contingent Remainders (1772), Mitford's Equity Pleading (1780), Jones on Bailments (1781), Sanders on Uses and Trusts (1791),

Fonblanque's Equity (1793–1794), Watson on Partnership (1794), and Chitty on Bills (1799). When American reports were only beginning and full libraries of English reports were by no means always accessible, such books were sometimes the best available repositories of the law. Some of these were by no means outstanding. But not infrequently they suggested even more insistently what was suggested in the Continental treatises on commercial law.

Also such books suggested like books to American lawyers and especially to American law teachers who needed books as the basis of teaching. It is suggestive that the Litchfield Law School, the first of our law schools in point of time, gave us two of our earliest text books of a modern type[41] and that the first fruit of the Harvard Law School was a treatise on real actions.[42] But much of the impetus for Anglo-American doctrinal writing came from reading the treatises of the Continental civilians. This was not merely because in the growth and absorption of the law merchant for want of other materials English as well as Americans had recourse to Continental books on commercial law. As they sought in the nineteenth century to organize and systematize the results of two centuries of growth, they looked to the civil law, upon which great systematists had been at work since Donellus in the sixteenth century, to furnish the general systemic ideas which were lacking in their own books. When Austin in 1826 was elected to the chair of jurisprudence in London, he felt bound to go to Germany, to study the civil law as a necessary preparation. He speaks of it in comparison with the common law as it stood in the English books of his time as "the realm of order and light." [43] Such was the impression it made also on two generations of American lawyers. One can understand why our law teachers set out to write such treatises and why when written their treatises were eagerly received.

But if the civilian treatises were a stimulus to American doctrinal writers, there was a fundamental difference from the start in the concreteness of our texts, and such is the Anglo-American frame of mind that this concreteness made for the success of books which had no claim to authority in the tradition they expounded. Gray tells us that "the common-law judge neglects imaginary cases but the civil-law jurist is in danger of neglecting real cases." He goes on to say: "It is comparatively easy to frame a rule when you can frame your own examples. Putting simple extreme cases, it is not difficult to draw a line between them. But when you come to the cases which real life presents, with their complications and limitations, the theorist is apt to divert his eyes." Again he says: "The judge has his facts given to him. The text writer makes his own typical cases, and the temptation to make them such as to render easy the deduction of general doctrines is well nigh irresistible." [44] There is much truth in this. But we must remember that Gray wrote in the nadir of American text book writing and grew up in the time of reaction from the extravagant estimate of the civil law which governed in the earlier part of the century. The civil law is a law of the universities. Its oracles have been law teachers. The common law is a law of the courts. Its oracles have always been judges. Our doctrinal writers could not write as oracles. They had to found their texts on the judicial oracles and those oracles were pronounced on the actual controversies of life, not on the hypothetical cases of the lecture room. Thus, the quality of concreteness was assured. It is suggestive that recent continental commentaries are making a large use of the decisions of the courts, as our texts had to do from the start.[45]

Yet doctrinal writing was able to achieve what it did for our law in its formative era largely because the best of the texts were the work of law teachers who had been required to formulate their ideas to the exigencies of teaching and submit them to critical hearers. The doctrinal treatises of the civil law had more than the traditions of Roman law and of the medieval universities behind their success in maintaining themselves as repositories of the law for centuries. But a taught tradition is the most enduring form of law. In this country the rise of law schools was steady after the first third of the nineteenth century and text books were the backbone of the instruction. Indeed, we did not learn to teach from the primary authorities as had been done in the medieval Inns of Court, till the last quarter of the century. By this time the text books had done their work and they passed out of the law school curricula in the era of systematizing and organizing of the law which followed.

What may we expect of doctrinal writing in our work of creative finding and shaping of law which is before us? The need of such books as those of the formative era is quite as great now as then, but for a different reason. Then the courts had little to go on and much to bring about. Now, they have too much to go on to permit judicial working over of all that must be treated, especially under the limitations that bind judicial action. They have increasingly less time for thorough first-hand work upon the vast mass of available material. Primarily they must render just decisions in the cases before them and the increasing complexity of cases adds to this task. Their dockets are congested. The labors of counsel, with the aid of the modern apparatus of digests and cyclopedias, put before them an enormous mass of authoritative matter in which they must find starting points for reasoning or analogies or rules. They cannot give the time to oral argument which was possible in the formative era.[46] If they are to do their work well there must be thorough working over of the law which has come down to us as only jurists and law writers can do it. And no one who has followed the history of American law can doubt that the jurists and law writers who are to do this will be law teachers. The experience of the American Law Institute confirms this.

Moreover a revival of doctrinal writing has begun in this generation. Such books as Wigmore on Evidence, Williston on Contracts, and Beale on the Conflict of Laws are permanent contributions to our law. They put the matured nineteenth-century law in form to be used in a new era of growth. So, too, of the work of the American Law Institute. For more than a generation the best energies of our law teachers have gone into the preparation of case books to be instruments of teaching. In many of these case books we may find creative work of the first order. They are necessary forerunners, under the conditions of today, of the great treatises that must come presently from the law schools. They have made possible the restatement which will be no small part of the basis of a juristic and thence a judicial new start. Whether as affording material for judicial decision or for administrative determination or for legislative lawmaking these summings up of the nineteenth-century law and placings of it in the order of reason with reference to the legal problems of the time will be invaluable. I am not in the least troubled that they have not essayed to give us an ideal body of precepts on each subject but rather have sought to present our law in its now stage of development at its best. We shall proceed more surely toward the ideal body of precepts for the future if we start from the best possible statement of what we have been able to achieve up to date.

And now let me bring these lectures to a close as I began them with a word about Livingston. Livingston did not act directly in any of the capacities in which men shaped our law in the formative era. He was not on the bench of an appellate court. His legislative service was political rather than lawmaking. He did not write great text books of the law to be cited by courts and studied by law students. But his drafts of penal legislation, his discussions of pleading and of evidence, and his writings on penal legislation and administration have had an influence on those subjects as they developed in American thought and American legislation quite comparable to that which the great doctrinal writers had on judicial decision. What Marshall and Kent and Story were to the law found and shaped by the judiciary, what Kent and Story were to our text made law, Livingston was to our penal legislation, which was not the least of the achievements of the formative era. When we begin presently to think in terms of a creative period, of a period of legal growth, I cannot doubt that Livingston will be held the great jurist of nineteenth-century America and one to rank with Bentham among English-speaking jurists.

[1] Pollock, First Book of Jurisprudence, 6 ed., 319, n. 1.

[2] Lord Eldon in Johnes *v.* Johnes, 3 Dow 1, 15; Ion's Case, 3 Den. C. C. 475, 488; Kekewich, J. in Union Bank *v.* Munster, 37 Ch. Div. 51; Note, 4 Law Quarterly Rev. 236; Note, *id.* 360–361; Note, 5 *id.* 229. Today English judges frequently refer to or even discuss the views of living text writers not on the bench. Bickersteth *v.* Shanu, [1936] A. C. 290, 297 (reference to article in 28 Halsbury, Laws of England, 798, that part by a living junior barrister); Russian and English Bank *v.* Baring Brothers & Co., [1936] A. C. 405, 443; Craven-Ellis *v.* Canons, [1936] 2 K. B. 403, 413; Bertram *v.* Wightman, [1936] 2 K. B. 521, 537 (book by living author who became a county court judge); Fender *v.* Mildmay, [1936] 1 K. B. 111, 117; Alexander *v.* Rayson, [1936] 1 K. B. 169, 190; Crozier *v.* Wishart Books Ltd., [1936] 1 K. B. 471, 476; Timpson's Executors *v.* Yerbury, [1936] 1 K. B. 645, 651 (Greene, L. J. refers to Withers on Reversions, 2 ed. 1933); Bruce *v.* Odhams Press, Ltd., [1936]

1 K. B. 697, 703, 714; With *v.* O'Flanagan, [1936] 1 Ch. 575, 580 (article in 20 Halsbury, Laws of England, 1 ed. 678, by a living barrister). These references are in marked contrast to the apologetic references to standard texts made by English judges a generation ago. There are in the volumes of the Law Reports cited many other references to articles in Halsbury's Laws of England which I have not included above because the authors were judges. Also court and counsel continually refer to old standard texts, *e.g.*, Brook's Wharf & Bull Wharf, Ltd. *v.* Goodman Bros., [1937] 1 K. B. 534, 543 (Leake on Contracts); Inland Revenue Commissioners *v.* Sharlston Collieries Co., [1937] 1 K. B. 590 (Gale on Easements); Boag *v.* Standard Marine Ins. Co., [1936] 2 K. B. 121, 124 (Arnould on Marine Insurance, Leake on Contracts, Phillips on Insurance); same case p. 127 (Phillips on Insurance cited by the court); St. Pierre *v.* South American Stores, [1936] 1 K. B. 382, 390 (Dicey on Conflict of Laws cited by Scott, L. J.); Timpson's Executors *v.* Yerbury, [1936] 1 K. B. 645, 650 (Lewin on Trusts cited by Greene, L. J.); In re Canning's Will Trusts, [1936] 1 Ch. 309 (Jarman on Wills cited by Farwell, J.); Shipley Urban District Council *v.* Bradford Corporation, [1936] 1 Ch. 375, 385, 387.

[8] When and where citation of English decisions was forbidden by statute or rule of court, they could be brought to the attention of judges by citing the text-books in which they were referred to or discussed. "It is not probable that the temporary exclusion of the judgments of Lords Kenyon, Ellenborough and Tenterden, or of the decrees of Thurlow and Eldon from the ear of Kentucky courts had any permanent effect on the jurisprudence of Kentucky. If the words of these sages of the law could not be read directly in the hearing of the judges, they would come to them indirectly through the pages of Kent and Story." Dembitz, Kentucky Jurisprudence, 8. Even English text-books were cited for the purpose. *Ibid.* note 7.

[4] See Holdsworth, Blackstone's Treatment of Equity, 43 Harvard Law Rev. 1.

[5] See my review, 24 Political Science Quarterly, 317.

[6] Walker, American Law, 1 ed. 61, 649.

[7] At the Harvard Law School till 1870, at Columbia till 1890, at Yale till 1916, at Virginia largely till the present. In the present century they have gone out almost entirely as the basis of teaching in the University Law Schools. See Reed, Training for the Public Profession of the Law, chap. 31; Redlich, The Common Law and the Case Method in American University Law Schools.

[8] English Law and the Renaissance, 18. See Pound, Taught Law, 37 Rep. Am. Bar Assn. 975 (1912).

[9] 2 Commentaries on American Law, 1–11.

[10] 1 Story, Commentaries on the Constitution of the United States, §§ 340, 348, 356.

[11] American Law, §§ 52, 626; 2 ed. § 659.

[12] Newbern, 1802. There was a translation by Evans reprinted in Philadelphia, 1826, 2 ed. 1839.

[13] By Cushing, Boston, 1839.

[14] Edited by Cushing, Boston, 1850.

[15] Transl. by Tudor, London, 1854.

[16] Ludlow *v.* Brown, 1 Johns. 1, 16; Suydam *v.* Mar. Ins. Co., *id.* 181, 191; Griswold *v.* New York Ins. Co., *id.* 205, 215; Patrick *v.* Hallett, *id.* 241, 242, 248, 249; Schmidt *v.* United Ins. Co., *id.* 249, 263, 265; Wheelwright *v.* De Peyster, *id.* 471, 479, 481, 482, 484.

[17] Watson *v.* Mar. Ins. Co., 7 Johns. 57, 62; Jumel *v.* Mar. Ins. Co., *id.* 412, 426; McBride *v.* Mar. Ins. Co., *id.* 431, 432, 433; Merritt *v.* Johnson, *id.* 473, 475; Dash *v.* Van Kleeck, *id.*, 477, 504, 505, 507.

[18] Jackson *v.* Jackson, 1 Johns. 424, 428, 430.

[19] Pitcher *v.* Livingston, 11 Johns. 1, 19–20.

[20] Gillet *v.* Mason, 7 Johns. 16.

[21] Campbell *v.* Messier, 4 Johns. Ch. 334, citing Pothier

repeatedly; Mowatt *v.* Wright, 1 Wend. 360, citing Pothier; Wheadon *v.* Olds, 20 Wend. 174, citing Pothier and Domat. In Merritt *v.* Johnson, 7 Johns. 473, 475, Pothier is cited in an action of trover. The last case of citation of French authorities on a common-law question, so far as I know, is Snedeker *v.* Waring, 12 N. Y. 170 (1854).

[22] Selection of Cases on the Law of Contracts, 156.

[23] Education of Henry Adams, chap. 5; Knight, Lord Monboddo and His Contemporaries, 4; Gray, Some Old Scots Judges, 43, 126.

[24] "The department of law where the peculiar genius of the Roman jurists found full scope is the law of obligations, the law of debtor and creditor, the law, in other words, which is most properly concerned with the mutual dealings between man and man; and here again it is more especially the law relating to those contracts, where not merely the expressed, but also the unexpressed intention of the parties has to be taken into account (the so-called bonae fidei negotia). And in regard to this unexpressed intention which is not, for the greater part, present to the mind of the party himself at the moment of concluding the contract, it was the Roman jurists who discovered it, and discovered it for all time to come, and enunciated the laws which result from its existence. This is a task which will never have to be done over again. And, at the same time, they clothed these laws in a form which will remain a model for all future ages. That is the reason why the law of obligations, and it alone — and more particularly the law of those bonae fidei negotia, and it alone — constitutes what is, in the truest and strictest sense, the imperishable portion of Roman law." Sohm, Institutes of Roman Law, transl. by Ledlie, 3 ed., 107.

[25] Const. N. Y. 1846, art. I, § 17, art. VI, § 25. Art. I, § 17 provides: "The Legislature, at its first session after the adoption of this Constitution, shall appoint three commissioners, whose duty it shall be to reduce into a written and systematic code the whole body of the law of this State,

or so much and such parts thereof as to the said commissioners shall seem practicable and expedient. And the said commissioners shall specify such alterations and amendments therein as they shall deem proper, and they shall at all times make reports of their proceedings to the Legislature, when called upon to do so; and the Legislature shall pass laws regulating the tenure of office, the filling of vacancies therein, and the compensation of the said commissioners; and shall also provide for the publication of the said code, prior to its being presented to the Legislature for adoption."

[26] Report of Joseph Story, Thereon Metcalf, Simon Greenleaf, Charles E. Forbes, and Luther S. Cushing, Commissioners to Take into Consideration the Practicability and Expediency of Reducing to a Written and Systematic Code the Common Law of Massachusetts or Any Part Thereof, 1836, reprinted by David Dudley Field, 1882.

[27] Act of December 19, 1860. See Code of Georgia, 1861, preface and Report of the Committee.

[28] Wigmore in The Future of the Common Law, 59; Gray, Nature and Sources of the Law, 2 ed. 275.

[29] The Civil Code of the State of New York, Reported Complete by the Commissioners of the Code, 1865. The Report, pp. v–ix, and Introduction, pp. xi–xxxii tell the whole story.

[30] *E.g.* France after the Revolution, Germany after 1871.

[31] Swift *v.* Tyson, 16 Pet. 1 (1842), now overruled in Erie R. Co. *v.* Tompkins, 58 Sup. Ct. Rep'r, 817.

[32] See Carter, Law: Its Origin, Growth, and Function, 307–309.

[33] Loyd, Early Courts of Pennsylvania, chap. IV.

[34] There is a full account in 1 Pomeroy, Equity Jurisprudence, 4 ed., §§ 311–321.

[35] "Each individual of the society has a right to be protected by it in the enjoyment of his life, liberty, and property according to standing laws." Massachusetts Bill of Rights (1780), § 10.

[36] Report of the Board of Statutory Consolidation on the Simplification of the Civil Practice in the Courts of New York, (5 vols., 1915–1919); Report of the Joint Legislative Committee on the Simplification of Civil Practice (1919); Report of the Commission on the Administration of Justice in New York State, 1934, 39–43, 241–366; Second Annual Report of the Judicial Council of the State of New York, 109–184, 213–222 (1936); Third Annual Report of the Judicial Council of the State of New York, 129–198, 277–327 (1937); Fourth Annual Report of the Judicial Council of the State of New York (1938).

[37] This method has not been confined to the United States. *E.g.* "The Law is stated as at November 1, 1937." 27 Halsbury, Laws of England, 2 ed. vii.

[38] Ordinance for the Government of the Territory of the United States North-West of the River Ohio, art. II; Ohio *v.* Lafferty, Tappen (Ohio) 81 (1817), overruled in Key *v.* Vattier, 1 Ohio 132, 144 (1823) and a long line of subsequent cases.

[39] American Law, 1 ed., § 52.

[40] Pleas of the Crown (1678).

[41] Reeve, Law of Baron and Feme, Parent and Child, Guardian and Ward, Master and Servant (1816); Gould, Principles of Pleading in Civil Actions (1832).

[42] Stearns, Summary of Law and Practice of Real Actions (1824).

[43] 1 Jurisprudence, 3 ed. 60.

[44] Nature and Sources of the Law, 2 ed., 277.

[45] *E.g.* in 12 Laurent, Droit Civil Français (1878), §§ 9–14 contain eighteen citations of commentators and writers and five citations of decisions. Today, 2 Planiol et Rippert, Traité pratique de droit civil Français (1933), §§ 24–28, dealing with the same subject, have eighteen citations of commentators and writers, but thirty-eight citations of decisions.

[46] See Pound, The Spirit of the Common Law, 8–9.

INDEX

INDEX

INDEX

INDEX

INDEX

INDEX

INDEX

INDEX

INDEX